NITROUS OXIDE SEDATION IN PEDIATRIC DENTISTRY

A CLINICAL HANDBOOK

SHREYAS SHAHID

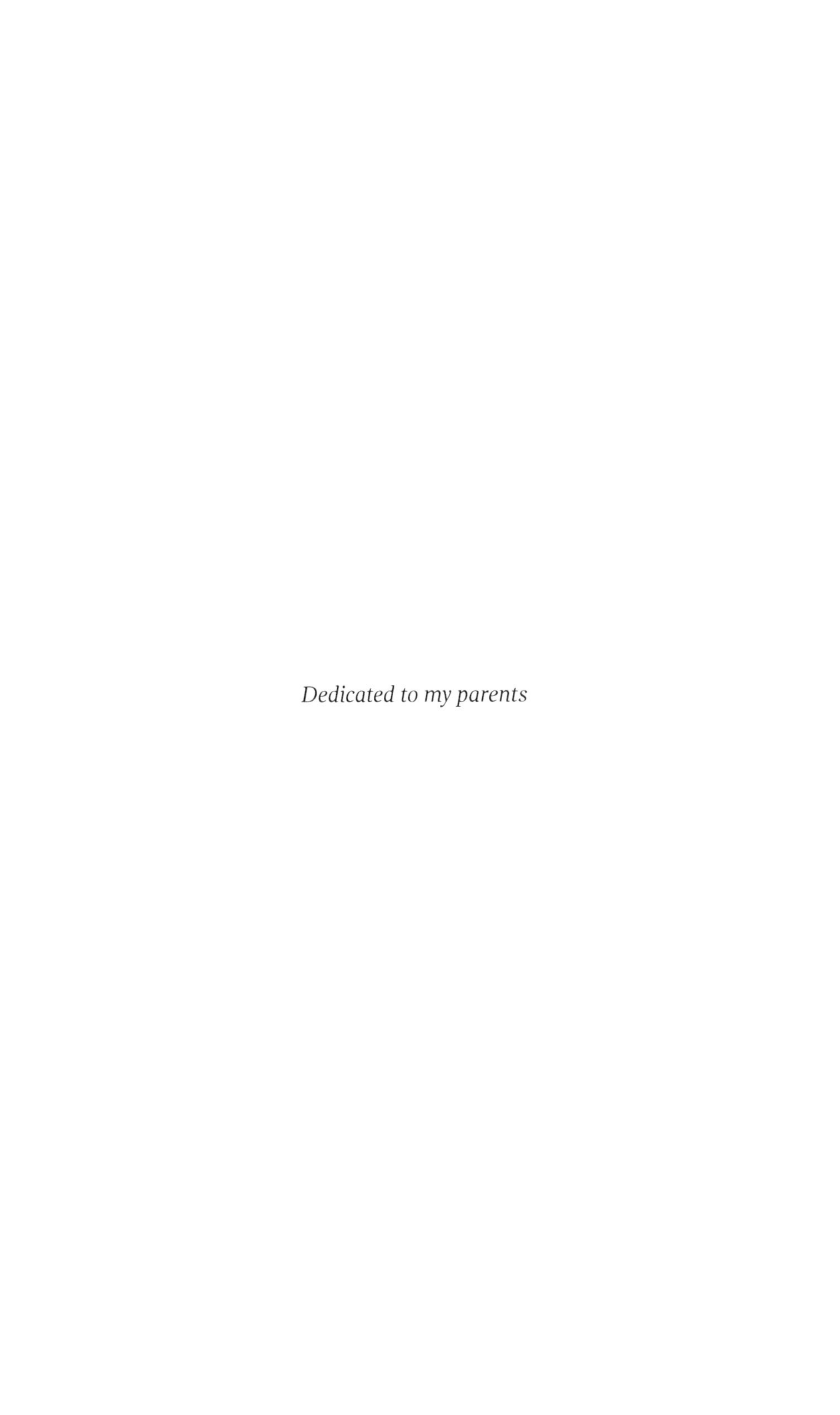

Dedicated to my parents

Contents

Foreword

It gives me immense pleasure to pen down this prologue to the book on Nitrous oxide sedation in pediatric dentistry. Being an author cum editor of an international book titled "Nitrous oxide in pediatric dentistry", I understand the importance and need for having textbooks on this topic.

Use of nitrous oxide in pediatric dentistry has been indispensable and over the last decade its use has been soaring in India. Pediatric dentists in India have begun to realize the role of nitrous oxide and how it serves as a true behaviour management tool by improving efficiency and efficacy as well as building a positive dental attitude at the same time. Having realized this, I prefer to designate nitrous oxide as the backbone of pediatric dentistry as it can change the face of a pediatric dental practice.

Being a pharmacological agent, many dentists shy away from using this technique. However, in the present era where parents look for comfort of their child and are not averse to the use of pharmacologic agent for getting dental treatment, nitrous oxide has an edge because of its anxiolytic and analgesic properties. It is time to integrate this technique in our practices.

This book is well planned with introduction to the concept of sedation, making it easier for the readers to clinically recognize different planes of sedation which is the basis for monitoring during nitrous oxide inhalation sedation. Technique of administration is also described in depth which would make the readers comprehend the entire process with ease and practise the same in their patients.

Dr. Shreyas Shahid is a dedicated pediatric dentist who is passionate about this topic. I could sense his zeal to learn about sedation during my course titled "The Nitrousoxide Masterclass" where he was one of the subjects. I am positive that his efforts of bringing out this book will help young dentists and also create more awareness on the topic of nitrous oxide sedation.

Dr. Kunal Gupta (MDS)

Author- “Nitrous oxide in pediatric dentistry: a clinical handbook”; Springer.

Director , Children’s Dental Center, Gurugram

Adjunct Faculty, Sharad Pawar Dental College, DMIMS, Wardha

Adjunct Faculty, People’s College of Dental Sciences, People’s University, Bhopal

Adjunct Faculty, D.Y. Patil Dental College, Pune

Acknowledgements

First and foremost, I would like to thank God for giving me the patience and strength to pen down this dissertation and for blessing me with all that I have in life.

I owe my sincere thanks to my guide, Dr. Shveta Sood for her constant guidance and encouragement throughout. She has been the pillar of support throughout my study and led me to develop a better understanding of the subject. I express my profound respect to my co-guide Dr. Naresh Sharma for his firm belief that nothing is impossible, his valuable advice, constructive criticism and his extensive discussions around my work.

I would also like to acknowledge the pivotal role of my family. I deeply thank my parents, Dr. Sanjay Subodh and Mrs. Sushma Sinha for their unconditional trust, timely encouragement and endless patience and my sister Sanjana Sahay who has been my inspiration and helped me at every stage of my personal and academic life. I owe everything to my family as they have longed to see this achievement come true.

I wish to express my heartfelt gratitude to my colleagues Dr. Akansha Thapliyal and Dr. M. Piraveen for their unwavering support and belief in me and for rendering me all the possible help. My sincere heartfelt thanks to my seniors Dr. Megha Sethi, Dr. Sabreen Gujral, Dr. Shruti Chopra and my juniors, Dr. Ronika Goyal, Dr. Tharani Thangaraju and Dr. Twinkle Chawla for always being there without any exception.

Last but not the least, many thanks to all my friends and colleagues who directly or indirectly motivated me and supported me in bringing this dissertation to fruition.

Shreyas Shahid

Faridabad, India
August 2022

CHAPTER I

Introduction

The child is nature's most benevolent creation. The process of a child's psychological development is dynamic, beginning at birth and moving through several phases in order and is manifested in the child's behaviour.[1] Fear, anxiety, and pain are continuously associated with dentistry. According to statistics, dental phobia affects 10–12 million people in the United States, and up to 35 million people avoid going to the dentist because of their anxiety. Pain and fear are connected. Due to the corresponding dread of pain, people will often endure extreme agony before seeking expert help.[2] Throughout childhood and adolescence, people experience fears. Fear is frequently seen as an essential and inevitable feeling that enhances the "fight or flight" reaction in dangerous situations, giving kids coping mechanisms for dealing with life's stresses.

It is therefore normal for youngsters to be frightened of a situation, particularly those which have harmed them before. Moreover dental fear and phobia represent a major barrier to dental care.[3] Most of the worries that children exhibit may have been learned either factually or subjectively. A child who has been mistreated or who has experienced excruciating pain in a hospital are examples of situations that would induce objective anxieties through direct physical stimulation. Subjective fears, such as hearing about painful dental experiences, are those that are founded on feelings and attitudes that have been given to the youngster by others.[4] Children who are afraid not only cause themselves indirect harm, but their behaviour in the dental office is also negatively impacted by their fear. Despite the correlation between oral behaviour management issues and dental anxiety, some studies show that children with dental fear can clinically differ from those with behaviour management problems.

Children with dental fear may be shy and passive during treatment while those with behavioural problems may be more outgoing and rebellious towards the treatment. Hence it becomes necessary to assess the level of fear and anxiety of the practitioner before embarking on any kind of responsibility for the child as a patient. Additionally, dental care for adults typically involves a one-to-one patient-dentist interaction; whereas, for children, it typically involves a one-to-two relationship with parents.[5] Thus, a child's behaviour is greatly influenced by the sentiments of their parents. Given that children's type of behaviour can never be used as an excuse for poor dental hygiene, providing complete dental care to young patients provides a unique difficulty.[6]

So how does one proceed with such challenges?

It is well accepted that in paediatric dentistry, initial treatment includes behaviour management. Whenever a kid's behaviour in the dental clinic cannot be controlled, doing any necessary dental treatment is difficult, if not impossible. Consequently, behaviour control is a foundational component of specialisation. When offering oral health care for babies, kids, and teenagers, dental health care providers may use a combination including both non-pharmacological and pharmacological behaviour counselling tactics, according to the American Academy of Pediatric Dentistry.[8] Several strategies can be used while keeping in mind the objectives of behaviour guidance, which include establishing communication, reducing fear, providing quality dental treatment, and encouraging a positive dental attitude in children. These can be broadly divided into basic and advanced behaviour guidance techniques.

The basic or non-pharmacological methods include communication, tell–show–do, reinforcement, distraction, live modelling, and contingent escape. These techniques are widely practised by dentists all over the world. Any of these fundamental methods, which serve as the cornerstone of all the management services offered by the dentist, can usually be used to control a recalcitrant child's behaviour. The most cautious behavioural strategy should be tried first. However, children could exhibit behavioural issues that call for more sophisticated methods. Use of physical restraints and the HOME techniques have been used but passive restraint may also prove to be insufficient for such patients.[1] Therefore, it becomes necessary to consider an adjunctive form of treatment, upon weighing the associated risks and benefits. The primary goal of the dentist's dental anxiety management strategies is to keep the youngster away from unpleasant and ineffective interactions with the dentist. The goal is to establish a setting that will support the growth of the child's confidence and enable the dentist to do operations with the least amount of interruption.[7]

Nitrous oxide sedation is a theory that has created new opportunities for handling recalcitrant children in the majority of allied healthcare disciplines, and it has rightfully grown in popularity among the busy modern dentists in developed countries.[6] Using a medicine or combination of medications to induce a condition of depression throughout the central nervous system is known as minimal sedation, allowing for the administration of treatment, but allowing for extensive verbal interaction with the patient throughout the sedation period. Minimal sedation for dental procedures should be possible using medications and methods with a margin of safety that makes unconsciousness unlikely.[9] Minimal sedation preserves the patient's capacity to maintain a patent airway reliably and independently.

• • •

References

1. Tandon S. Textbook of Pedodontics. 2nd ed. India: Paras Medicals; 2008. P. 1-3.
2. Anesthesia and sedation in the dental office, J Am Med Assoc 254:1073 1985.

3. Beaton L, Freeman R, Humphris G. Why are people afraid of the dentist? Observations and explanations. Med Princ Pract. 2014;23(4):295-301.
4. Marwah N. textbook of Pediatric dentistry. 4th ed. New Delhi: Jaypee Brothers Medical Publishers; 2018. P. 206-207
5. McDonald RE, Avery DR, Dean JA. Dentistry for the child and adolescent. 10th ed. Missouri: Mosby Elsevier; 2016.
6. Shashikiran ND, Reddy SV, Yavagal CM. Conscious sedation- An artist's science! An Indian experience with midazolam. J Indian Soc Pedod Prev Dent 2006 Mar;24(1):7-14.
7. Folayan MO, Faponle A, Lamikanra A. A review of the pharmacological approach to the management of dental anxiety in children. Int J Paediatr Dent 2002; 12:347-5.
8. The Reference Manual of Pediatric Dentistry 2020-2021. P. 7-9
9. Kapur A, Kapur V. Conscious Sedation in Dentistry. Ann Maxillofac Surg. 2018 Jul-Dec;8(2):320-323.

CHAPTER II

Objectives For Sedation In Pediatric Dentistry

Paediatric dental care sedation goals take the child's and the dentist's requirements into account.[1]

Factors which consider the need of the child

- Reduce anxiety and pain perception during the procedure
- Make the procedure easier
- Prevent the occurrence of dental anxiety and fear

Factors which consider the need of the dentist

- Facilitate the completion of dental operations
- Reduce stress and ugly emotions
- Prevent "burn-out" syndrome from occurring

• • •

References

1. Hallonsten AL, Jensen B, Raadal M, Veerkamp J, Hosey MT, Poulsen S. Guidelines on Sedation In Pediatric Dentistry. 2003.

CHAPTER III

Minimal sedation

Sedation has been described in a variety of ways over the years, but in 1971, following the Third Pain Control Conference sponsored by the American Dental Association (ADA), American Dental Society of Anesthesiology, and American Association of Dental Schools, the "Guidelines for Teaching the Comprehensive Control of Pain and Anxiety in Dentistry" were published. These recommendations established a benchmark for dental staff training in this patient management area.[1]

Over the years, there have been several times when the guidelines have been revised, most recently in 2007 when the House of Delegates of the ADA passed two documents that represented significant revisions to the guidelines, among them changes to the terms used to describe the various categories of levels of sedation. The Guidelines were most last updated in 2016.[1]

The following gives the definition of minimal sedation according to the revised ADA guidelines.

Minimal sedation (this definition was previously associated with anxiolysis)—"a minimally depressed level of consciousness that retains the patient's ability to independently and continuously maintain an airway and respond appropriately to physical stimulation or verbal command and that is produced by a pharmacological or nonpharmacological method or a combination thereof. Although cognitive function and coordination may be modestly impaired, ventilatory and cardiovascular functions are unaffected."[1,2]

The foundation for safety comes from two elements in the definition of minimal sedation:

1. The patient keeps their airway open, which is a skill that may be lost when one descends to deeper levels. If the second condition is satisfied, airway maintenance and reflexes can be presumed to be

normal.

2. Patients will react adequately to verbal or physical commands.[2]

	Minimal Sedation (Anxiolysis)	Moderate Sedation/ Analgesia (Conscious Sedation)	Deep Sedation/ Analgesia	General Anesthesia
Responsiveness	Normal response to verbal stimulation	Purposeful* response to verbal or tactile stimulation	Purposeful* response after repeated or painful stimulation	Unarousable, even with painful stimulation
Airway	Unaffected	No intervention required	Intervention may be required	Intervention often required
Spontaneous ventilation	Unaffected	Adequate	May be inadequate	Frequently inadequate

Table 4.1 Continuum of Depth of Sedation: Definition of General Anesthesia and Levels of Sedation/Analgesia. (*Reflex withdrawal from painful stimulus is not considered a purposeful response.)[5]

Objectives of Minimal Sedation

1. Having a responsive patient with reduced fear or anxiety is the aim of minimal sedation.

2. The patient's mood needs to be changed: The main goal of minimal sedative treatments is to change the patient's mood such that a procedure that was previously psychologically unfavourable now becomes easily acceptable.

- Minimal sedation aims to get rid of anxiety and dread in order to help control pain reaction.
- Sedative approach is not used to punish or control pain. By carefully incorporating localised analgesia, pain perception can be controlled.

3. The patient must stay cooperative: It goes without saying that the patient's cooperation is essential when regional analgesia is being utilised to control post-operative pain. However, patient cooperation will come once the anxious patient has been comforted

and his attitude improved.

4. The pain threshold should be raised: Although regional analgesia is frequently used by dentists to manage post-operative pain, it is desirable to use minimal sedative medications that also raise the pain threshold at the CNS system level.

5. All protective reflexes must be active at all times: While aware, the patient will always keep his airway open and free of secretions.

- There is no chance of soft tissue obstructing the airway, which can happen when consciousness is lost.
- In addition, the respiratory system is taken into consideration. The patient's reflexes will keep them from becoming hypoxic.

6. The patient's vital signs should only show slight variations:

- The physiology of the patient is not altered to the same degree as it is while they are unconscious.
- With proper drug doses and rates of administration, minor changes in vital signs we observed before, can reach normal limits because a previously fearful or apprehensive patient is now calmed.
- The calming effect produced may therefore result in a lowering of a previously elevated pulse rate or blood pressure seen in apprehensive individual.

7. Amnesia may be present to some extent: This depends on the medications used and the dosage. If the patient is conscious, this can be done quickly.[3,4]

Properties of a Sedative

- Alleviate fear and anxiety.
- Produce a degree of amnesia and analgesia.

- Suppress vomiting reflexes but not protective reflexes.
- Prolong potential operating time.
- Be rapidly effective.
- Have a sufficiently long effect which then quickly wears off.
- Have no side effects.
- Be safely and easily administered by the operator.
- Special procedures or precautions before or after use are not required.
- Selection of the proper agents and administering them in incremental doses while observing the patient's reaction a dentist can develop a technique that is unique to each patient physical needs.[3,4]

• • •

References

1. Malamed SF. Sedation-e-book: a guide to patient management. Elsevier Health Sciences; 2017 May 3.
2. American Dental Association: Council on Dental Education: Guidelines for teaching pain control and sedation in dentists and dental students, as adopted by the Oct. 2007 ADA House of Delegates, Chicago, 2007, The Association.
3. Craig D, Boyle C. Practical conscious sedation. Quintessenz Verlag; 2019 Sep 16.
4. Bennett CR. Conscious-sedation in dental practice. Mosby Incorporated; 1978.
5. American Society of Anesthesiologists Task Force on Sedation and Analgesia by Non-Anesthesiologists: Practice guidelines for sedation and analgesia by non-anesthesiologists. Anesthesiology 96:1004–1017, 2002

CHAPTER IV

Routes of Drug Administration

There are numerous ways that medications could be given. The primary 10 of these pathways are employed in dentistry, while the primary 13 are used in the practice of medicine. In veterinary medicine, the intraperitoneal route is employed. These routes are as follows: [1]

1. Oral
2. Rectal
3. Topical
4. Sublingual
5. Intranasal (IN)
6. Transdermal
7. Subcutaneous (SC)
8. Intramuscular (IM)
9. Inhalation (pulmonary)
10. Intravenous (IV)
11. Intraarterial (IA)
12. Intrathecal (within the spinal cord)
13. Intramedullary
14. Intraperitoneal

Oral Route

The most popular method of medication administration is oral. It is superior to parenteral medication administration in many ways, making it better for a variety of scenarios requiring the control of pain and anxiety. This path has some substantial drawbacks as well, which must be highlighted. Advantages include 100% patient acceptability, easy administration, and a reasonable level of safety.

Patients nowadays are habituated to ingesting their medicines. Adult patients who choose other administration methods than oral are quite uncommon. However, the younger youngster frequently proves to be a reluctant participant in oral medication administration. Any mode of medication administration can result in unwanted drug side effects, including overdosage, idiosyncrasy, and allergies, however, it is more difficult to discern these reactions when a drug is taken orally. When they do happen, they often don't cause as severe of reactions as those that result from parenteral injection. This is not meant to imply that circumstances that pose a risk to life do not develop after the oral medication intake. Indeed, reports of cardiac arrest and allergy following oral medication delivery exist.[2, 3]

Oral medication delivery has several drawbacks, including a protracted incubation period, unpredictable drug sorption, an incapacity to quickly produce the intended pharmacological effect, and an extended duration of action. These serious drawbacks contribute to restricting the clinical application of the oral route in the management of discomfort and worry in an outpatient setting. Most orally taken pain and anxiety-relieving medications extend their duration of effect by about three to four hours. This time frame is not suitable for the majority of dental procedures since the patient will continue to be affected by the drug well after the procedure and well into the recovery period, making it impossible for them to leave the dentist's clinic alone. Patients using oral CNS depressants must be cautioned about operating potentially hazardous machinery or operating a vehicle, and children must be watched until the effects of the medication wear off.

For the control of anxiety prior to surgery as well as the management of postoperative pain, oral medications may be used safely and successfully. Due to significant drawbacks, the oral route of medicine delivery is not highly advised for use on a regular basis in the treatment of intraoperative pain and anxiety.

Rectal Route

It's employed in paediatric dentistry, wherein it is more typical to run into kids who can't or won't take oral drugs.[4,5]

The term "parenteral route of drug administration" refers to drug delivery techniques in which the medication is absorbed directly into the systemic circulation without first passing via the gastrointestinal system. The oral and rectal routes through which medications are transferred first from the gastrointestinal tract into the enterohepatic circulatory system before entering the systemic circulation are known as "enteral modes of drug administration". The benefits and drawbacks of drug administration via the rectal route are identical to those of drug administration via the oral route. When a medicine is taken via the rectal route, it is less probable that adverse pharmacological effects would be seen and will be less severe. Additionally, it has a protracted latent period, unpredictable drug absorption, and delayed action times.

Topical Route

Although local anaesthetics applied topically can produce anaesthesia in tissues devoid of a layer of keratinized skin, such as the mucous membranes of the mouth, nose, throat, trachea, bronchi, oesophagus, stomach, urethra, bladder, vagina, and rectum, they do so at the expense of very poor drug absorption through the entire skin.[6,7]

A highly effective and efficient way to lessen some of the anxiety and discomfort that could be associated with the administration of injectable local anaesthetics is topical anaesthesia, which is utilised in dentistry.[8,9] The use of medications other than local anaesthetics topically is not very common.

Sublingual Route

It is possible to deliver some medications sublingually, which allows for blood absorption through the oral cavity's mucous membranes. Triazolam for moderate sedation is one such instance of a medication used clinically that is administered sublingually.[10]

Sublingual medication delivery has the advantage of bypassing the enterohepatic circulation and allowing the drug to enter the systemic circulation directly. This prevents the drug from going through the hepatic first-pass metabolism, which occurs before the drug has a chance to reach its target organ, such as the encephalon, by entering the systemic circulation.[11]

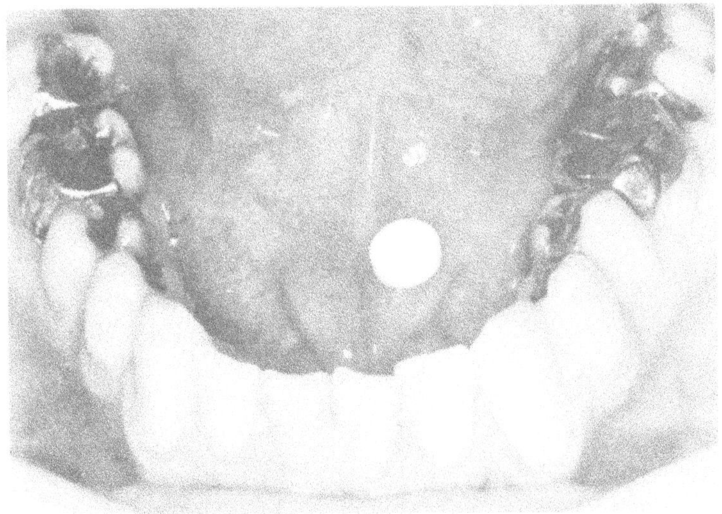

Fig. 5.1 Glyceryl trinitrate tablet placed in the sublingual region.[22]

Intranasal Route

Intranasal medications have mostly been used in paediatrics to avoid the necessity for oral or injectable medication administration in recalcitrant and/or reluctant kids.[12] Intranasal medicines bypass the enterohepatic circulation and are absorbed directly into the systemic circulation. Clinical studies have shown that intranasally delivered medications almost have the same absorption and bioavailability as those given intravenously, with peak plasma levels arriving 10 minutes after delivery.[13,14]

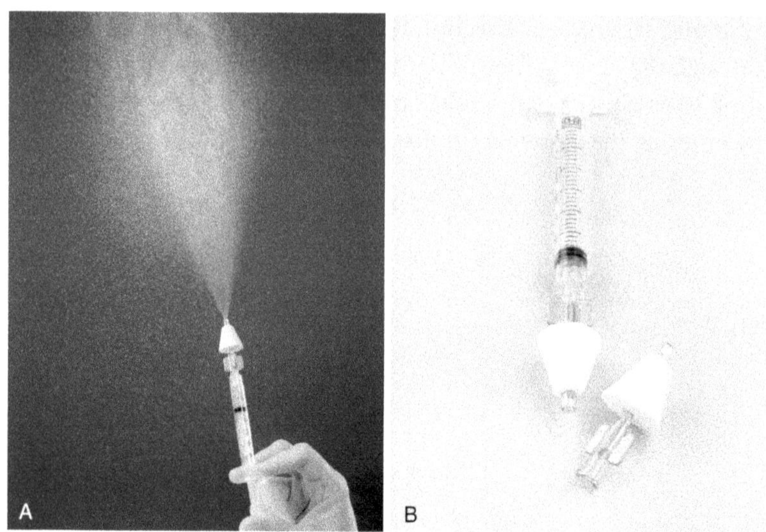

Fig. 5.2 Aerosol spray on IN syringe. (Source: www.intranasal.net.)

Transdermal Route

Bypassing the GI tract and avoiding injection, the transdermal method allows for medication administration.[15] When a lengthy course of medication therapy is required, transdermal drug administration is considered. Although transdermally given analgesics are rarely used in dentistry, they may be helpful in certain situations, such as those following surgery. Transdermal medication administration may have drawbacks such as unpleasant skin reactions at the application location and a decrease in drug responsiveness.[16,17]

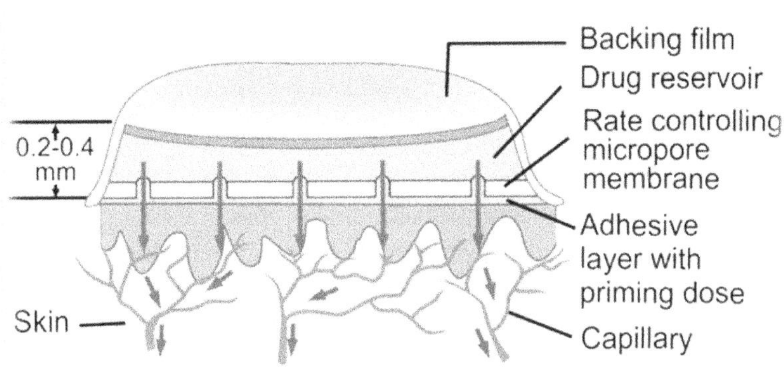

Fig. 5.3 llustration of a transdermal drug delivery system.[21]

Subcutaneous Route

A medication is injected into the subcutaneous tissues via the subcutaneous route just beneath the skin. It is helpful for administering hypnotic, narcotic, and non-volatile, water- or fat-soluble medications.[18] The usefulness of this method in dentistry is constrained by the sluggish rate of absorption following a subcutaneous injection. Other quicker-acting and more manageable methods are favoured and are available.

Intramuscular Route

A parenteral method that is superior to enteral methods in a number of ways, the intramuscular route of medication delivery is unquestionably effective in the treatment of pain and anxiety. The intramuscular route, however, pales in significance when compared to other parenteral modes of delivery, particularly inhalation and intravenous ones. The oral, intranasal, inhalation and intravenous routes are the most popular ones utilised in dentistry, whereas the intramuscular route is the least frequently employed. The intramuscular route of administration has advantages over enteral methods, including a quicker commencement of action (around 10 minutes) and a quicker onset of the maximum clinical effect (roughly 30 minutes). The other benefit is that drugs are typically more effectively absorbed into the CVS after intramuscular delivery as opposed to oral administration. As opposed to most other procedures, patient cooperation is not as important here. Younger paediatric patients who are unable to demonstrate desire during medicine delivery benefit most from this feature. Only a brief period of restraint is necessary when administering the injectable medication to the children.

The 10-minute latent period of intramuscular injection is a drawback that renders titration impossible. Also, if an overdose or other difficulties occur, it is unfeasible to swiftly annul the effects of medication. Patients might not want to consent to the injection required to administer the medication. The action's protracted length (about 2 to 4 hours or more) necessitates that the patient is escorted by a trusted companion when leaving the dentist's office, and there is a chance that the drug or the needle may cause harm to the tissues at the injection site. However, with individuals who have impairments and youngsters who are unwilling or uncooperative, procedures that call for any amount of patient compliance are expected to prove hard to apply successfully, and the intramuscular route or, more frequently now, the intranasal route may be the only available method of sedation. The patient may only be able to receive general anaesthesia as a form of treatment.[19]

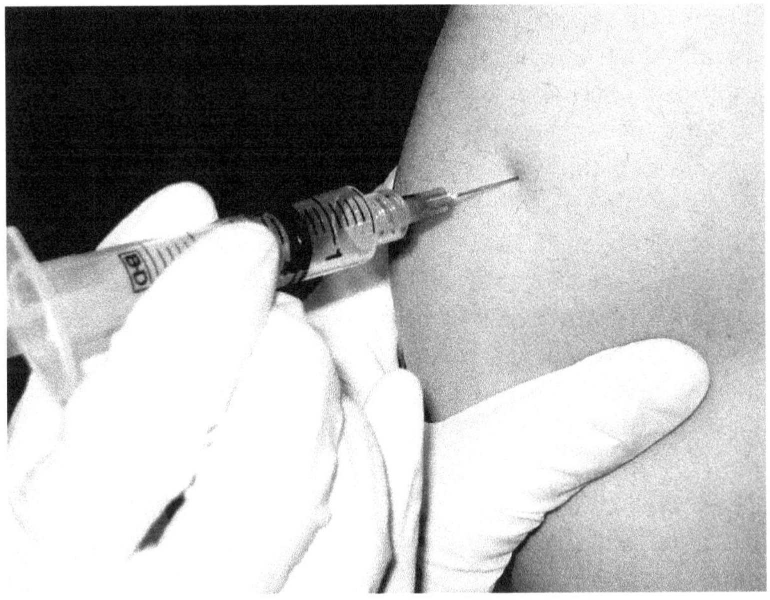

Fig. 5.4 Area to be injected is grasped with one hand, holding tissue taut, while the syringe, held in a dartlike grasp, is inserted to the proper depth.[23]

Intravenous route

The most efficient way to guarantee consistent and appropriate sedation in almost all patients is by intravenous medication administration. Drug blood levels that are effective are quickly reached. The capacity to immediately increase a drug's activity if necessary and its short latent time of 20 to 25 seconds are two benefits of intravenous drug administration. One drawback of medications given intravenously is that no medication can be made to behave differently once it has been injected. The significant clinical effects and early commencement of action of intravenously injected medications might cause more pronounced issues such as overdosage, side effects, and allergy symptoms. The use of these medications, as well as the identification and management of any associated adverse reactions and crises, must thus be thoroughly explained to the entire office personnel.

Venepuncture can only be successful with the patient's participation. Intravenous sedation is rarely recommended or tried in these unruly youngsters because many kids won't allow venepuncture to be done. Contrarily, a compliant child who is prepared to remain calm and allow venepuncture to take place typically does not necessitate a method like intravenous sedation for dental care. The use of inhalation sedation or another sedative method may be used in conjunction with intraoral injections of local anaesthetics. Patients with physical and mental impairments, however, are frequently suitable patients for intravenous sedation. These children may not be cooperative through dental treatment, but after being sedated, they frequently collaborate extremely well.[19]

Inhalation (Pulmonary) Route

Many different gaseous substances can be inhaled to create drowsiness or general anaesthesia. The use of N_2O and O_2 by inhalation is essentially interchangeable in dental practice. Since 1844, both medicine and dentistry have used N_2O, the first general anaesthetic. Inhalation sedation is perhaps the most popular sedation method in pediatric dentistry.[20]

The inhalation route's latent time was shown to be quite brief. The fastest onset of clinical effect is provided by the inhalation route. The medication enters the CVS quickly after passing via way of the mouth, nose, trachea, and lungs. Clinical effects from some inhalation drugs, including N_2O, can be felt as soon as 15 to 30 seconds after inhalation. Many believe that N_2O-O_2 inhalation sedation is the best sedative method currently available because it allows for titration due to the brief latent period. Additionally, should it be necessary, the person administering the gases has the capacity to immediately reverse the effects of the medicine. As a result, the inhalation route is the only one where the pharmacological effect can be quickly changed to either deepen or shallow drowsiness. Recovery from mild sedation brought on by inhalation is also swift and complete. Fast recovery is desirable in dentistry because it enables the dentist to release all N_2O-O_2 recipients from the clinic. The patients can resume their everyday activities without any obstacles. It is a benefit that N_2O-O_2 inhalation sedation alone possesses.

The use of the inhalation method has some similar drawbacks. Given that N_2O is not a particularly effective anaesthetic, there will be a certain proportion of patients in whom this approach will not be successful in producing the required effects when administered with at least 20 per cent O_2. The successful use of inhalation sedation depends on patient cooperation; a lack of this collaboration results in a disadvantage. The management of wayward kids and kids and adults with impairments is where this is most frequently seen. In a dental environment, children should be able to breathe through their nostrils. Inhalation sedation is very uncomfortable for dental patients who can't breathe via their nose. The size and cost of the apparatus as well as the further instruction and costs necessary for the safe delivery of N_2O-O_2 are a few minor drawbacks of the inhalation route.

The method of choice for most dental procedures requiring intraoperative anxiety control is N_2O-O_2 inhalation sedation. N_2O-O_2, however, does not reliably manage pain, therefore it is not recommended to use it as a local anaesthetic in place of a painkiller.[19]

Route of administration	Disadvantages over nitrous oxide sedation
Oral	• Cannot titrate the drug • Delay in onset • Varying response due to difference in gastric absorption • No oral reversal drug present • Longer pre-procedural fasting required
Intramuscular	• Difficult for patients who are needle phobic • Can cause muscular pain • Over sedation possible • Longer pre-procedural fasting required
Intravenous	• Difficult for patients who are needle phobic • Over sedation possible • Longer pre-procedural fasting required
Intranasal	• Difficult to administer • Can cause burning sensation in nasal mucosa • Over sedation possible

Fig. 5.5 Disadvantages of other modes of sedation over inhalational mode (nitrous oxide).[24]

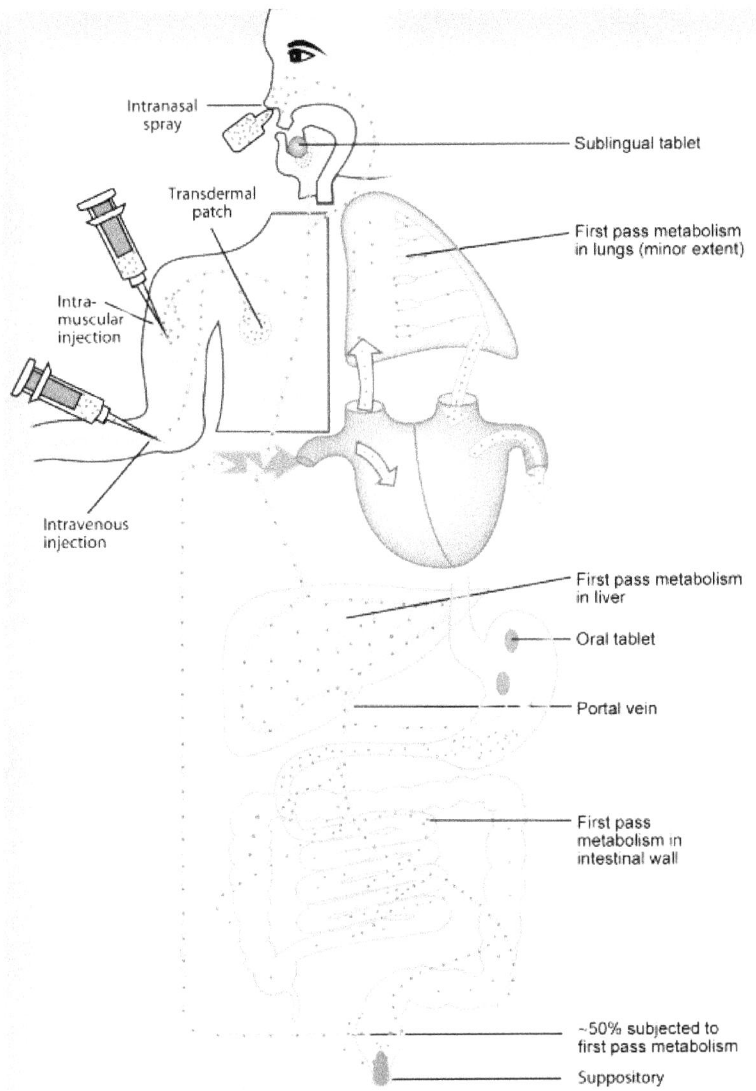

Fig. 5.6 Various routes of drug administration, vascular pathway of drugs absorbed from various systemic routes of administration and sites of first pass metabolism.[21]

• • •

References

1. Malamed SF. Sedation-e-book: a guide to patient management. Elsevier Health Sciences; 2017 May 3.
2. Chugh SS, Socoteanu C, Reinier K, et al: A community-based evaluation of sudden death associated with therapeutic levels of methadone. Am J Med 121(1):66–71, 2008.
3. Gill CJ, Michaelides PL: Dental drugs and anaphylactic reactions: report of a case. Oral Surg 50:30, 1980.
4. Flaitz CM, Nowak AJ, Hicks MJ: Evaluation of anterograde amnesic effect of rectally administered diazepam in the sedated pedodontic patient. J Dent Child 53:17, 1986.
5. Jensen B, Matsson L: Benzodiazepines in child dental care: a survey of its use among general practitioners and paediatric dentists in Sweden. Swed Dent J 25(1):31–38, 2001.
6. Ernst AA, Marvez-Valls E, Nick TG, et al: TAC (lidocaine-adrenaline-tetracaine) versus TAC (tetracaine-adrenaline-cocaine) for topical anesthesia in face and scalp lacerations. Am J Emerg Med 13(2):151–154, 1995.
7. Erdurmus M, Aydin B, Usta B, et al: Patient comfort and surgeon satisfaction during cataract surgery using topical anesthesia with or without dexmedetomidine sedation. Eur J Ophthalmol 18(3):361–367, 2008.
8. Carr MP, Horton JE: Clinical evaluation and comparison of 2 topical anesthetics for pain caused by needle sticks and scaling and root planning. J Periodontol 72(4):479–484, 2001.
9. Deepika A, Rao CR, Vinay C, et al: Effectiveness of two flavored topical anesthetic agents in reducing injection pain in children: a comparative study. J Clin Pediatr Dent 37(1):15–18, 2012.
10. Pickrell JE, Hosaka K, Jackson DL, et al: Expanded studies of the pharmacokinetics and clinical effects of multidose sublingual

triazolam in healthy volunteers. J Clin Psychopharmacol 29(5):426–431, 2009.

11. Kontinen VK, Maunuksela EL, Sarvela J: Premedication with sublingual triazolam compared with oral diazepam. Can J Anaesth 40(9):829–834, 1993.
12. Heard C, Smith J, Creighton P, et al: A comparison of four sedation techniques for pediatric dental surgery. Paediatr Anaesth 20(10):924–930, 2010.
13. Rey E, Delaunay L, Pons G, et al: Pharmacokinetics of midazolam in children: comparative study of intranasal and intravenous administration. Eur J Clin Pharmacol 41:355–357, 1991.
14. Walbergh EJ, Wills RJ, Eckhert J: Plasma concentrations of midazolam in children following intranasal administration. Anesthesiology 74:233, 1991.
15. Asmussen B: Transdermal therapeutic systems: actual state and future developments. Methods Find Exp Clin Pharmacol 13:343, 1991.
16. Parker JO: Nitrate tolerance: a problem during continuous nitrate administration. Eur J Clin Pharmacol 38(Suppl 1):21, 1990.
17. Hogan DJ, Maibach HI: Adverse dermatologic reactions to transdermal drug delivery systems. J Am Acad Dermatol 22(Pt 1):811, 1990.
18. Dugas R: Subcutaneous drug administration. An alternative used in palliative care. Can Fam Physician 47:266–267, 2001.
19. Bennett CR. Conscious-sedation in dental practice. Mosby Incorporated; 1978.
20. Haupt M: Project USAP 2000—Use of sedative agents by pediatric dentists: a 15-year follow-up survey. Pediatr Dent 24:289–294, 2002.
21. Tripathi KD. Essentials of pharmacology for dentistry. Jaypee Brothers Medical Publishers; 2020 Nov 23.
22. Florence AT, Salole EG, editors. Routes of Drug Administration: Topics in Pharmacy. Elsevier; 2013 Oct 22.

23. Malamed SF. Medical emergencies in the dental office, ed 7, St Louis, 2015, Elsevier Mosby.
24. Gupta K, Emmanouil D, Sethi A, editors. Nitrous Oxide in Pediatric Dentistry: a clinical handbook. Springer Nature; 2019 Dec 4.

CHAPTER V

History Of Nitrous Oxide Anaesthesia-Discovery And Development

"The search will continue. It is older than history. It is not satisfied and will not be suppressed.
-Edwin Hubble (1889-1953)"

It is simple to overlook what early medical experts went through to create routine techniques like N_2O/O_2 sedation in today's era of sophisticated medicine and cutting-edge technology. It took bravery for the early scientists to experiment with unfamiliar, potentially hazardous materials and ad hoc tools. They frequently gave up their health and security to promote science. We are able to deliver analgesia and anaesthesia today in a safe and effective manner thanks to the boldness of these early medical explorers. Although the field of dentistry has a long history of being associated with pain, researchers have continued to look for ways to lessen patients' discomfort. Before the invention of anaesthesia, early surgeries were performed under conditions that would be seen as cruel by modern standards.

The history of how nitrous oxide inhalation sedation came to be employed in modern medicine and dentistry is fascinating because it also tells the tale of how the art and science of anaesthesiology developed. The most widely used inhalation anaesthetic in dentistry and in all medicine is nitrous oxide, which is credited with being the first anaesthetic to be used clinically for the relief of pain. As hard as it is to believe, neither O_2 nor N_2O was known. The English gentleman Sir Joseph Priestley is credited with discovering both N_2O and O_2. German O_2 had been created by Stephen Hales in 1727, but he failed to recognise it as an element, and Sir Joseph

Priestly and Scheele are credited with making the discovery in 1772. By burning ammonium nitrate combined with iron fillings and purifying the gas by running it through distilled water, Priestly discovered nitrous oxide.[1]

Fig. 3.1 Joseph Priestly who also discovered oxygen is credited with isolating nitrous oxide.[11]

A field of science known as pneumatic medicine was established in the late 1700s. Bristol, England's Pneumatic Institute, founded by Thomas Beddoes, became one of the key research hubs for the newly created gaseous vapours. At this point, Priestly's contemporary Sir Humphery Davy developed an interest in the study of these gaseous agents.

Fig. 3.2 Humphry Davy, described the capacity of nitrous oxide to prevent pain, suggesting its use in surgical procedures, but no one took up his suggestion.[11]

Davy became the first person to continuously inhale pure N_2O in England in 1798, even though N_2O gas was thought to be the cause of several illnesses and fatal disorders. Davy found the experience to be enjoyable; he felt ecstatic and like smiling instead of suffering some terrible fate. He carried on his research, claiming that it resulted in the "most voluptuous pleasures." Other words he used to describe his N_2O experiences were "ideal existence" and "overwhelming joy." Davy issued a booklet containing the findings of his research in 1800.[2] He also suggested in this book that nitrous oxide inhalation might be utilised to lessen pain during surgical procedures. Despite this crucial observation, the rest of the medical community did not give this agent considerable consideration or use it to relieve pain during surgery. N_2O experiments persisted for the next 40 years, although not for medicinal purposes. Under the guise of a doctor, Samuel Colt, a 19-year-old famous for his firearms, started putting on N_2O sideshows on street corners. These performances were promoted as a chance for young people to have fun at night and "laugh, sing, speak, or fight." Using N_2O has become a popular pastime at social gatherings and on college campuses. At many lectures, it was the main demonstration.[1]

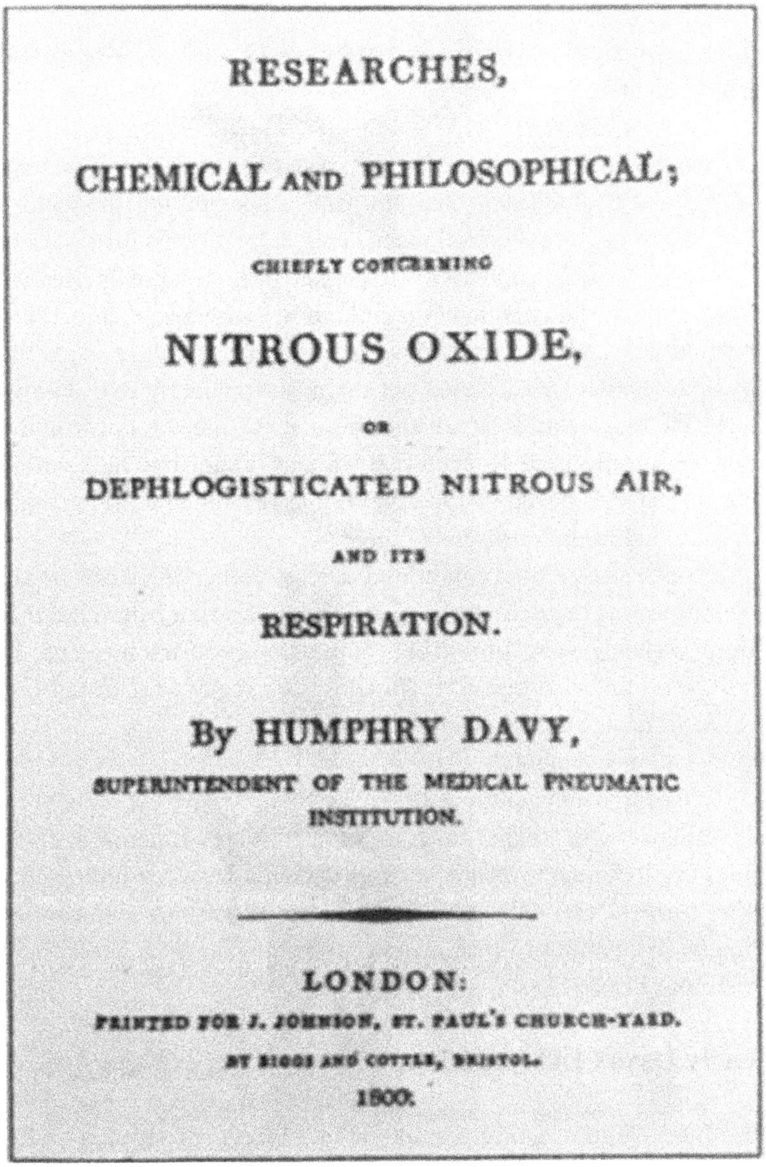

RESEARCHES,

CHEMICAL AND PHILOSOPHICAL;

CHIEFLY CONCERNING

NITROUS OXIDE,

OR

DEPHLOGISTICATED NITROUS AIR,

AND ITS

RESPIRATION.

By HUMPHRY DAVY,

SUPERINTENDENT OF THE MEDICAL PNEUMATIC INSTITUTION.

LONDON:

PRINTED FOR J. JOHNSON, ST. PAUL'S CHURCH-YARD.

BY BIGGS AND COTTLE, BRISTOL.

1800.

Fig. 3.3 The first book written on nitrous oxide by Sir Humphry Davy.[11]

The medical world ignores N_2O as a potential anaesthetic

Although careless usage of N_2O persisted in the early nineteenth century, the medical profession was desperate for painkillers. Patients frequently died following surgical treatments for a variety of causes. It was imperative to reduce pain because ineffective infection control frequently resulted in subsequent infections. Amputations, teeth extractions, and abscess drainings were the procedures that were carried out the most frequently. The sutures were the biggest medical advancement at the time. A hot iron did not have to be used to cauterise wounds, and a boiling solution did not have to be applied to amputation-remaining extremities in order to induce hemostasis.[3]

Patients frequently committed suicide rather than endure an operation without pain medication. The methods of pain relief that were available were unreliable, imprecise, cumbersome, and, at best, just somewhat effective. Numerous strategies were tested:

A. Securing a patient using corporeal force

B. Opium/ alcohol

C. Ice/ tourniquets

Patients who might undergo surgery were sometimes given difficult decisions to make, such as deciding between undergoing pure torment and unbearable pain during surgery or enduring an illness or condition that would probably cause a protracted, torturous death.

Early Days (1844-1860)

Gardner Quincy Coltonconsidered a pioneer of nitrous oxide anaesthesia was born on Feb 7, 1814, in Georgia, Vermont. He was a former medical student who has failed to complete his studies and later majored in chemistry and natural philosophy in 1842. Colton continued to research and teach on the effects of nitrous oxide gas after learning about them during his medical studies.

Fig. 3.4 Gardner Quincy Colton.[11]

On December 10, 1844, Professor Colton gave a popular science talk about December 1844 at the Exhibition in Hartford, Connecticut, at the suggestion of one of his students. It served as a demonstration of the exciting benefits of N_2O inhalation.[4] In this performance, audience members were asked to participate in a presentation of the effects of nitrous oxide gas as it was described and shown. On this particular evening, Dr Horace Wells, a local dentist, was in the crowd. Although he had a successful dental practice, his heightened sensitivity made it impossible for him to handle the excruciating suffering of his patients.[2] Store clerk Samuel Cooley offered to get nitrous oxide during the demonstration. Cooley instantly became inebriated and started racing about the stage after breathing 100% nitrous oxide using a spigot connected to a bladder sack that contains gas. Wells saw that despite Cooley's hindlimb striking the table's side forcefully during this period, he carried on as usual. After the event, Wells got in touch with Cooley, who said he was not aware of the injuries.

Fig. 3.5 Horace Wells.[11]

Wells contacted Prof. Colton about this incident and whether a tooth could be extracted while under the influence of nitrous gas. He also requested that a nitrous oxide demonstration be set up the following day at Wells' dental clinic. On December 11, 1844, at the office, a hesitant Colton assisted Dr John Riggs in extracting a third molar tooth from Dr Wells while acting as his anesthesiologist.

Wells said that he had been completely unconscious of the process and that there had been zero pain involved after recouping from the gas‘ effects. Wells said this was the "greatest discovery ever made," and he suggested that this marked the start of a new era of "tooth-pulling." Prof. Colton taught him how to create N_2O, and he soon started applying it to his dentistry practice.

The Horace Wells experiment

Wells was able to get approval to show his recently discovered technique to the faculty and students at the prestigious Harvard Medical School thanks to his friendship with William TG Morton. Wells employed N_2O during extractions on multiple patients with outstanding success. Dr Wells gave N_2O using a freshly created inhaler to a volunteer patient who was a medical student. Wells had to take away the inhaler to pick up the tools needed to perform the extraction as the patient became asleep. The crowd began to publicly disapprove of Wells once the patient began to cry during the extraction, thinking that the treatment had failed. Wells was eventually forced to leave the demonstration hall, utterly humiliated by the failure of his endeavour. The patient claimed that when he first awoke, he was completely oblivious of what had happened, had no memory of the surgery, and had no memory of yelling out loud. Wells was called a "charlatan" and a "fake" since his admission was unsuccessful and arrived too late.[5]

There were a number of justifications offered at the time for this "failed" demonstration. The first is that Wells had to perform twin roles as an anesthesiologist and a surgeon. The second is the idea of biological variation, and the third is an ignorance of the varied anaesthesia levels. Unfortunately, Wells’ demonstration is a failure, and as a result, he loses his professional reputation and stops practising dentistry. He stopped promoting the clinical use of N2O and instead began experimenting with various inhalants, quickly developing a chloroform addiction.

In May 1848, a buddy begged Horace Wells to provide him with a container of sulfuric acid so he can give it to the courtesan who damaged his clothing. Wells refused to provide this further when approached by a friend. But after returning to Broadway in New York for a few days, He hurled sulfuric acid at two more courtesans while under the influence of chloroform. For these actions, he was apprehended and jailed. Horace Wells killed himself on May 30th, 1848, at the age of 33, by using a razor to cut his femoral artery in the left limb.[5]

Fig. 3.6 Crying patient during demonstration by Horace Wells at the Harvard Medical School.[13]

In the history of the development of inhalation anaesthesia, Horace Wells will forever be remembered by the dental and medical history as the discoverer of anaesthesia. . He is still acknowledged as the **"Founder and Father of Inhalation Anaesthesia"**.

One of the first organisations to give Wells "all the honours" for discovering and effectively using the uses of gases or vapours to do surgeries without feeling pain was the Medical Society of Paris in France.[4] Every doctor in Hartford, Connecticut, signed a statement saying that Wells was the original discoverer of anaesthesia.[16] He received official recognition from the American Dental Association (ADA) in 1864 and the American Medical Association (AMA) in 1870. The AMA reaffirmed Wells' valuable contribution to the medical field on the original exhibition's 100th anniversary (1944), and various dental and anesthesiology organisations reiterated their affirmations during the profession's 150th anniversary (1994).[4] The Baltimore College of Dentistry, the first dental school in the nation, awarded him a posthumous Doctor of Dental Surgery degree in 1994. On the fifty-fifth anniversary of Wells' discovery, an association of dentists and physicians called the Horace Wells Club was established in Hartford, Connecticut. Since the beginning, each year they get together to celebrate this great philanthropist and improve the science of anaesthesia. The Horace Wells Club supports scholarships for Connecticut dentistry students and cares for the Horace Wells statue in Bushnell Park in Hartford. Additionally, they provide a commendation award each year to a person who has excelled in the field of sedation and shown leadership. To honour Horace Wells, the Hartford Medical and Dental Societies, the Connecticut Dental Association, and the Horace Wells Club have held fundraising activities, generate money for the restoration of Wells' grave in Cedar Hill Cemetery, and assist regional groups that work to prevent suicide.

The Late 1800s- Resurgence of N_2O

Gardner Quincy Colton, who had first given Wells the notion to employ N_2O, reintroduced nitrous oxide to the dental healthcare system in July 1863. Thus, the effects of nitrous oxide and its application in medicine and dentistry started gathering recognition only after 20 years of the ill-fated demonstration by Dr Wells.

Colton, together with his colleagues Dunham and Joseph H, founded "dental institutes" in locations around the United States and collaborated on tooth extractions under nitrous oxide anaesthesia throughout the summer of 1863. The patient inhaled 100% nitrous oxide through his or her lips while the administrator supported the patient's nose. Colton quickly rose to the top of the anaesthesia hierarchy. Colton had delivered nitrous oxide to 193800 individuals (ranging in age from 3 years to 90 years) by 1881, 18 years after his reintroduction of N2O, and had then documented them.[9]

Colton had a background in chemistry and medicine, and he was unmatched in his ability to administer nitrous oxide, but he was still ignorant of the underlying chemical and physiological effects of the gas. However, Colton produced his nitrous oxide for 20 years using a crude device that he had created not long after starting to use the gas as an anaesthetic. It is thought that without him, this substance would not have returned to the fields of anaesthesia and dentistry. Soon the news of the potential of this gas spread like fire and its various applications were seen in surgeries performed under 100% N_2O. Mastectomy and limb amputation was performed by Dr J.M. Carnochan and Evans performed an eye operation using nitrous oxide anaesthesia. As soon as the potential of this gas became known, it spread like wildfire, and many uses for it were discovered in operations carried out in a nitrogen dioxide environment. Dr J.M. Carnochan performed a mastectomy and limb amputations, and Evans underwent an eye operation under nitrous oxide anaesthesia.

Nitrous oxide was only utilised at 100% concentration up to 1868. Vermont-born doctor Edmund W. Andrews (1824–1904) practised medicine. He was the first to combine N_2O and O2. The Oxygen Mixture: A New Anaesthetic Combination, which he later published in Chicago Medical, was his contention that this mixture was safer and more enjoyable.[2] Paul Bert predicted in 1969 that breathing pure N_2O for longer than two minutes would result in suffocation. He created a device that can provide nitrous oxide at a rate of 75% and oxygen at a rate of 25%.[10] After that, liquid

N_2O was made commercially available to the dentistry and medical industries in England in 1872, making its use considerably secure and quite practical. Doctors and dentists now do not have to create their own gas at the danger of introducing pollutants into N_2O. To give N2O/O2 in predetermined ratios, Sir Frederick Hewitt created the first effective anaesthesia machine in 1887. In Liverpool, England, dental cavity preparation began with N_2O - O_2 analgesia in 1889. Low-speed handpieces, contaminants, and inadequate local anaesthetic procedures all contributed to several issues that made N_2O-O_2 less effective by the 1890s.

The Twentieth Century

This era mainly dealt with the development of the N_2O-O_2 delivery machines and types of equipment along with its ever-increasing use worldwide. A device that could deliver N2O O2 and other inhalation chemicals was introduced in 1902 by the Cleveland Manufacturing Company. Also in 1910, E.I. McKesson revealed the first oscillatory flow apparatus with accurate N_2O-O_2 % control. Most dentists who used N_2O during the 1930s and 1940s did so in the previously established 80:20 ratio of N_2O-O_2, but several continued to utilise 100 per cent N_2O anaesthesia. As the 1940s went on, gas purity improved, and the calibre of gas delivery equipment improved, leading to an increase in the number of dentists employing N_2O.

The way N_2O was utilised changed when lidocaine, the first of the more recent local anaesthetics, entered clinical usage in 1945. Its major purpose has changed from the elimination of pain to the control of anxiety and the induction of relaxation. The renowned textbook Practical Anaesthesia for Dental and Oral Surgery by Dr Harry M. Seldin was released in 1947. It included the characteristics and application methods of nitrous oxide-oxygen anaesthesia. N_2O was used in dentistry more regularly in the 1950s and 1960s. With the introduction of improved local anaesthetics for surgical pain control, the use of 100 per cent N_2O was rapidly declining, and

N_2O-O_2 quickly gained popularity as a treatment for nervous dental patients. Even dental schools started offering regular inhalation sedation classes. One of the pioneers in introducing these courses was Dr Harry Langa. Relative Analgesia in Dental Practice: Sedation with Nitrous Oxide, a classic book he wrote, was released in 1966. Additionally, he had taught the procedure to more than 6000 dentists in a secure manner.[2]

In 1977, the American Dental Association conducted one of the early studies on the use of N2O. Only 35% of dentists were using N_2O at the time in their offices. This proportion increased to 56% in 1994. Unfortunately, these surveys did not particularly include paediatric dentists. N2O was a common pharmacological agent used by 89 per cent of paediatric dentists, with the majority employing it more than five times per week, according to a 1996 report by Wilson et al. Four surveys on paediatric dentists' use of sedatives conducted between 1985 and 2000 show similar trends. Dentists used N2O in a variety of ways, despite its increased use, which did not reduce practice variation.

It should be emphasized that for most of its first years of dental application, N_2O was used as general anaesthesia. Patients were rendered unconscious for 1 to 2 minutes, initially using N_2O only and later combined with O_2. The operation was performed quickly and with anticipation that the patient would regain consciousness shortly thereafter. Administration of N_2O remained potentially lethal until its usage shifted from anaesthesia to analgesia and sedation in the second half of the 20th century which could be achieved with much lower dosages. Learning further about nitrous oxide usage and how it might be more practical in today's modern dental and medical practice is still a growing trend.

• • •

References

1. Stanley F.Malamed 2nd edition
2. Langa H, WB Saunders: Relative analgesia in dental practice: inhalation analgesia with nitrous oxide, Philadelphia, 1968.
3. Fenster JM: How nobody invented anesthesia, Am Herit Invent Technol 12(1):24, 1996.
4. Jacobsohn PH: Dentistry's answer to "the humiliating spectacle": Dr. Wells and his discovery, J Am Dent Assoc, 1994, 125:1576.
5. Menczer LF, Mittleman M, Wildsmith JA: Horace Wells, J Am Dent Assoc, 1985 110:773.
6. Jacobsohn PH: What others said about Wells, J Am Dent Assoc, 1994, 125:1583.
7. Chancellor JW: Dr Wells' impact on dentistry and medicine, J Am Dent Assoc, 1994, 125:1585.
8. MacAfee KA: Nitrous oxide. I. Historical perspective and patient selection, Compend Contin Educ Dent,1989, 10:352.
9. Clark MS, Brunick AL. Handbook of nitrous oxide & oxygen sedation 3rd ed. Missouri: Mosby Elsevier; 2002.
10. Malamed SF. Sedation: A guide to patient management. 4th ed. Missouri: Mosby; 2003.
11. Eger II EI, Saidman LJ, Westhorpe RN, editors. The wondrous story of anesthesia. Springer New York; 2014.
12. Smith W.D.A. A history of Nitrous oxide and oxygen anesthesia. Part V: The crucial experiment, its eclipse, and its revival. British Journal of Anesthesia 1966; 38: 143–156
13. George S. Bause; Horace Wells' "Humbug Affair" Occurred at Massachusetts General Hospital? Humbug!. Anesthesiology 2013;119(5):1009–1010

CHAPTER VI

Properties of Nitrous Oxide

The person administering N_2O-O_2 sedation to children needs to be knowledgeable about the substance's physical characteristics, pharmacokinetics, and dynamics.

Pharmacokinetics is the study of how medications behave in the body over time, including how they are absorbed, distributed, and localised in tissues, how they are biotransformed, and what physiological effects they have. The investigation of a substance's biochemical and physiological properties as well as its mechanism of action, including how those effects relate to the chemical makeup of the drug and how they affect the action of other medications, is known as pharmacodynamics. Numerous beneficial characteristics of nitrous oxide stand out in an ambulatory context.

Physical Properties

- Nitrous oxide is an inorganic inhalational agent which has a slightly sweetish odour.
- It is non-irritating to tissues and is also non-allergenic.
- The boiling point of the gas is -89°C indicating that at ambient temperature, it is gaseous. It becomes liquid when coarcted into cylinders.
- The molecular weight is 44 and its specific gravity is 1.43 which is greater than that of water (S.G. = 1) and pure oxygen (S.G. = 1.1).
- N_2O itself is non-flammable but supports combustion. The gas decomposes if it encounters a volatile material or flame that is hotter than 650°C. A strong chemical response, such as an explosion, will take place if the breakdown takes place at a raised temperature and increased pressure, such as inside a cylindrical

canister or pipeline. When N_2O is present around an open fire, the flame burns brighter.[1]

Chemical Properties

- Nitrous oxide also known as di-nitrogen monoxide is made up of 2 nitrogen atoms and 1 oxygen atom.
- Its Merck's Index is 6751.
- It is a chemically diagrammed stable linear compound with the formula N=N=O. Other names for it include factitious air, laughing gas, and hyponitrous acid anhydride.

Pharmacology

Pharmacokinetics: It involves the body's absorption, transfer, metabolism, and disposal of medications.[2] N_2O is inhaled by the mouth and nose, moved through the respiratory tract, and then quickly absorbed into the pulmonary circulation in the alveolar sacs of the lung.[3]

Agents that are inhaled, like N_2O, act on the body by travelling through a partial pressure gradient, or from a higher level to a lower level pressure gradient. The pace at which the agent passes the pulmonary membrane and enters the bloodstream is indicated by the variations in partial pressures of a gas (N_2O) and a liquid (blood). The blood-gas partition coefficient is what's known as this. The alveolar membrane is easily crossed by N_2O. Low N_2O partition coefficients also exist between tissues, muscles, and fats. As a result, equilibrium happens quickly because tissues cannot store N_2O. The idea of the concentration effect of N_2O on induction was first put forth by Eager.[2] When a patient receives a high concentration of N_2O, the concentration effect happens (70 per cent N_2O). Frequently, these concentrations are given during general anaesthesia. However, this effect is not substantial at lower concentrations. The "second-gas effect" refers to the phenomena whereby the second gas can be sucked in much more quickly due to N_2O's quick absorption. This enables the simultaneous administration of N_2O and small doses of a stronger anaesthetic. 90% of it is removed through the lungs without going through any biotransformation after being digested by the liver. Small amounts (0.004 per cent) are digested in the digestive system.

Pharmacodynamics: The assessment of a medicine's biochemical and physiological properties as well as its mode of action, along with the connection amongst those actions, results, and the drug's chemical makeup, is known as drug metabolism. The chemical mechanism of nitrous oxide's action is still partially understood. Therefore, the pharmacodynamics of nitrous oxide is still unknown. The minimum alveolar concentration (MAC), which is the quantity of medicine required to stop activity in 50% of subjects reacting to surgical incision, is used to evaluate the drug's potency.[4]

MAC for N_2O is 1.04 + 0.10 atmospheres. The average dose required 38% in patients undergoing various dental treatments supplementing local anaesthesia. The analgesic potency of nitrous oxide is proportional to inhaled concentration. A small but statistically significant reduction in reported pain and an improved tolerance can be experimentally demonstrated in subjects receiving 30 to 33% nitrous oxide during electrical tooth pulp stimulation or cutaneous radiant heat application. Therefore, nitrous oxide is most useful in the office setting as a mild sedative with anxiolytic and some analgesic properties supplementing the use of local anaesthetic.[4]

Concentration	Pain threshold	Pain tolerance
Baseline	21.8 + 9.8	34.6 + 16.3
15% nitrous oxide	25.6 + 9.9	39.4 + 17.1
30% nitrous oxide	29.6 + 9.4	44.6 + 16.7
45% nitrous oxide	31.2 + 9.3	47.2 + 16.4

Table 6.1. Effect of nitrous oxide concentration on pain threshold and tolerance during electrical tooth pulp stimulation in human volunteers. The number represents µAmps at which subjects reported incipient pain.[4]

Interaction With The Body

- **Cardiovascular system:** N_2O has generally shown to be mildly cardio-tonic, and it has no notable deleterious effects on CVS.[6] At a ratio of 80% N_2O to 20% O_2, a little decrease in myocardial contractions is produced, but there are no modifications to cardiac function. When there is no hypoxia, blood pressure stays constant. There is evidence of cutaneous vasodilatation, which results in some flushing and perspiration. Patients who are nervous about getting venepuncture can benefit from vasodilatation.

- **Respiratory system:** As for the pulmonary epithelium, it is not irritated. As a result, it should be given to asthmatic patients without running a higher risk of bronchospasm. Instead of the direct effect of N_2O on the respiratory system, the rate of breathing is more likely to be caused by the sedative alleviation of anxiety (steady and deeper) or the approach to the excitement stage (fast and shallow).[3]

- **Central nervous system:** N_2O can lower CNS, just as other sedatives. The mechanism, however, is uncertain. There is a very slight memory impact. Except in cases of hypoxia, the postrema of the medulla is unaffected.[3] The frequency and voltage alterations in the EEG are influenced by the N_2O dosage. Additionally, pneumo-cephalography instances revealed considerable intracranial pressure increases due to the fast substitution of N_2 with N_2O in air gaps.[2] Parbrook classified the effects of nitrous oxide into four zones of analgesia and gave descriptive analogies for each zone.

1. Zone 1:(6-25%) Subject with some analgesia with full verbal communication
2. Zone 2:(26.45%) Patients with psycho- logically detached, dreamy or seemingly inebriated.
3. Zone 3:(46.65%) Patients were markedly amnesic and responded to verbal commands but in a deeper plane sometimes lost consciousness.
4. Zone 4: (66.85%) was considered as light general anaesthesia.[5]

Within 40 seconds after N_2O was started; subjective symptoms of tingling and warmth were reported. Alterations in psychomotor function were observed with the use of all concentrations. A peak effect was reached in five minutes of administration with unresponsiveness to verbal commands.[4]

- **Hematopoietic system:** Methionine synthetase, an enzyme involved in the metabolism of vitamin B_{12}, is inhibited by N_2O, which impairs bone marrow function. When laboratory animals are exposed to N_2O for an extended period, this can disrupt DNA synthesis and result in symptoms resembling pernicious anaemia. Transient bone marrow depression can result from prolonged exposure to N_2O.[3]

- **Gastrointestinal Tract:** On GIT, nothing significant has happened. N_2O may still be utilised to effect without an increased chance of overdose or unfavourable reaction even in the presence of hepatic impairment.[3]

- **Kidneys:** No discernible impact on urine volume, content, or kidney function.[3]

- **Skeletal muscle:** Skeletal muscle relaxation is not brought about by N_2O. Any effects are linked to the reduction of anxiety rather than to the direct effects of N_2O.[3]

• • •

References

1. McDonald RE, Avery DR, Dean JA. Dentistry for the child and adolescent. 10th ed. Missouri: Mosby Elsevier; 2016.
2. Clark MS, Brunick AL. Handbook of nitrous oxide & oxygen sedation 3rd ed. Missouri: Mosby Elsevier; 2002.
3. Malamed SF. Sedation: A guide to patient management. 4th ed. Missouri: Mosby; 2003.
4. Trieger N, Loskota WJ, Jacobs AW, Newman MG. Nitrous oxide—a study of physiological and psychomotor effects. The Journal of the American Dental Association. 1971 Jan 1;82(1):142-50.
5. Jastak JT. Nitrous oxide in dental practice. International anesthesiology clinics. 1989 Jan 1;27(2):92-7.
6. Shashikiran ND, Reddy SV, Yavagal CM. Conscious sedation- An artist's science! An Indian experience with midazolam. J Indian Soc Pedod Prev Dent 2006 Mar;24(1):7-14.

CHAPTER VII

Functional Anatomy and Physiology of Respiratory System

Any inhalation technique Anatomical systems related to air intake, air output, and gas exchange are affected by sedation. Knowing the fundamental anatomy and physiology of the respiratory system, especially the changes in children, is crucial for inhalation sedation, such as using nitrous oxide-oxygen.

Normal physiology and respiratory mechanics

More than 300 million alveoli are found in the respiratory region of the lungs, where the gaseous exchange across the alveolus, as well as the pulmonary capillaries, as well as the pulmonary capillaries, occurs. Gases are breathed through the nose and/or mouth and transferred to the respiratory zone of the lungs. The body's densest capillary network is formed by pulmonary capillaries, which makes them special. The pulmonary capillaries' surface area in adults is about 770 metres square, or 40 times the size of the body. These capillaries contain 100 to 300 ml of blood at any given moment.[1]

Differences in pressure within the respiratory system led air to migrate from the atmosphere outside to the level of the alveolar-capillary membrane. From one area of higher pressure to another, gases travel. Partial pressure is the term for the pressure that gases dispersed in water or bodily fluids also produce. The pressure inside the pleural cavity is negative just prior to inspiration: - 5 cm of water, which is the typical resting pulmonary pressure. The lung's innate propensity to retract inward causes this negative pressure. The chest cavity expands and the muscles of inspiration contract as inspiration begins, further boosting the negative pressure within the thorax, i.e., 7.5 cm of water. Alveoli enlarge, as a result, creating a little amount of internal pressure that pulls air into the alveoli. Tidal volume (500 ml in a normal adult) develops as air enters the system, signalling the end of inspiration. As the pleural pressure begins to return to its resting value of - 5 cm of water, this causes the positive pressure inside the alveoli during exhalation and the maximal expiratory flow out of the respiratory system. Two features of the mechanics of respiration are crucial in nitrous oxide sedation.

1. Minute ventilation refers to the volume of air entering each minute. It is computed by dividing the rate of respiration by the tidal volume. The amount of gas to be administered to the patient is determined by minute ventilation in nitrous oxide-oxygen sedation. A lack of it can make breathing difficult and provide the impression of suffocation. While an excessive amount of volume could waste gas.
2. The volume of air that enters the alveoli in a minute is known as alveolar ventilation. It is derived by deducting the minute ventilation from the minute dead space volume. Remember that not all of the nitrous oxide that is inhaled makes it into the alveoli to participate in the gas exchange.

Muscles involved in process of breathing are:

1. Diaphragm (primary)
2. Intercostals (primary)
3. Abdominals (accessory)
4. Scalene (accessory)
5. Sternocleidomastoid (accessory)
6. Other back muscles (accessory)[1]

The main muscle responsible for silent breathing is the diaphragm. 350 cc of air enter the lung with diaphragm displacement of 1 cm vertically downward each during normal breathing. When breathing quietly, only the diaphragm is active.

Exchange of Gases: Gas exchange occurs at the alveoli–capillary membrane. Oxygen and carbon dioxide diffuse through this thin membrane. This depends on-

- The partial pressure of each gas
- Concentration gradient across the membrane
- Area available for diffusion

GAS	INSPIRED AIR	ALVEOLAR AIR	EXPIRED AIR
O_2	20.94	14.2	16.3
CO_2	0.04	5.5	4.0
N_2	79.02	80.3	79.7

Table 7.1. The composition of atmospheric gas.

These gases work together to provide a pressure of 760 mm Hg at sea level. Partial pressure is the name for the pressure of each separate gas. The difference in partial pressure determines the rate of gas exchange. The gas quickly dissolves in blood until the partial pressure in blood equals that of the alveoli if the gas entering the alveolus has a higher partial pressure than that present in the capillary.

GAS	Air (mm Hg)	Alveolus (mmHg)	Arterial Blood (mm Hg)	Venous Blood (mm Hg)
O_2	158.2	103	100	40
CO_2	0	40	40	46
N_2	596.5	570	573	573
H_2O Vapour	5.0	47	47	47

Table 7.2. Partial pressure of different gases and inhalation agents[2]

When delivered, N_2O/O_2 reaches significant concentrations in the alveoli. As a result, N_2O has high partial pressure and diffuses quickly into the capillaries. However, because it is insoluble in blood components, equilibrium is quickly reached (3 to 5 mins). As N_2O is transported to the brain, this rapid motion keeps going. It starts off quickly. When N_2O is stopped, the opposite is also true; the capillary N_2O pressure quickly rises above the alveoli pressure, causing the blood's N_2O to reach the alveoli fast and be expelled. Diffusion hypoxia is the term for this phenomenon, which occurs when the body uses the remaining trace amounts of O_2 for metabolism but substitutes them with N_2, which depletes the O_2 supply and lowers O_2 blood saturation.

Differences between child and adult respiratory system

The anatomy and physiology of adults and children differ in a number of ways. Children shouldn't be treated as miniature grownups. The paediatric respiratory system is defined by several characteristics that increase the likelihood that the kid would have respiratory failure. They consist of the following.:

Anatomic differences:

- A child has a relatively large and posterior placed tongue with large heads and short necks.
- A child's trachea, oropharynx, and nostrils are all quite small. Mucosal inflammation can make it difficult to breathe.
- Salivary secretions of a child are more pronounced.
- When compared to C5-6 in adults, the larynx is located more ventrally at the level of C3-4. The cricoid cartilage's sensitive mucous membrane, not the glottis as it is in adults, forms the narrowest portion in children up to the age of 8 to 10. The

larynx of a child is funnel-shaped, but that of an adult is more cylindrical. The epiglottis is long, stiff, formed like a U, and extends posteriorly at a 45-degree angle.

- The trachea has a narrow diameter of about 6 cm and measures 4 to 5.7 cm from the glottis to the canine as opposed to 6 to 8 cm in adults. It is more likely to become blocked.
- Alternative treatment alternatives should be considered for patients whose tonsillar tissue covers more than 50% of the pharyngeal space due to an elevated risk of respiratory obstruction. Children have a lower tolerance for breathing difficulties. Therefore, abrupt apnoea is more of an issue for children. Children have a lower functional reserve because their thoraxes are smaller and have less expansion capacity.
- The thorax is considerably shorter and much softer in newborns and young children than in the lungs. Children have a lower functional reserve because their thoraxes are smaller and have less expansion capacity.
- Infants have fewer alveoli i.e., about 20 million at the time of birth which, by the age of 8, the number gradually rises to 300 million.[3]

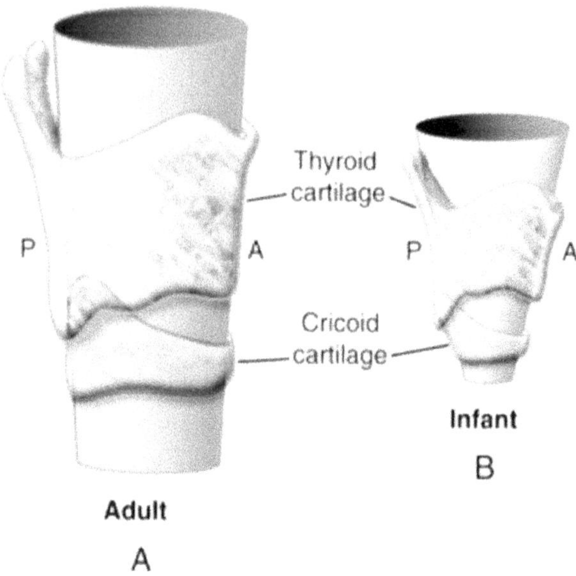

Fig 7.1 Configuration of the larynx in an adult (a) and an infant (b). Note that in both adult and infant the larynx is somewhat funnel-shaped, with an exaggeration of this shape in the infant.[5]

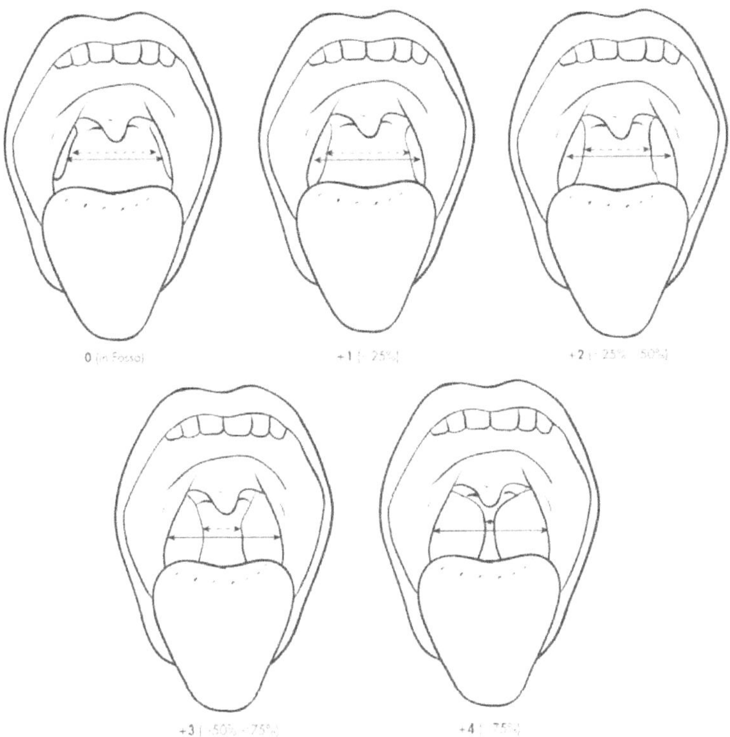

Fig 7.3 : A standardized system for evaluation of tonsillar size. Classification of tonsil size should be completed for all patients before sedation. Patients classified as +3 or greater are at increased risk for developing airway obstruction[4]

Physiological differences:

1. **Compliance**: A child's pulmonary compliance or elasticity is low and it increases as the child grows older. In young children, almost all the work of breathing is done by the diaphragm.
2. **Pulmonary volumes**: Compared to its size, a child's lung has a volume equal to that of an adult. Due to their higher respiratory

rates, children's alveolar ventilation, which ranges from 100 to 150 ml/kg/min, is two times higher as that of adults. The functional residual capacity (FRC) is the sum of expiratory reserve and residual volume. It acts as a buffer to maintain arterial oxygen during breathing. It is less in children. Now the ratio of AV: FRC is 5:1 in a child as compared to 1.5:1 in an adult. As a result, the changes in concentration of anaesthetic agents are reflected very quickly in a child's arterial oxygenation during breathing. Moreover, the supine position required for dental procedures further reduces the FRC. Any reduction in FRC can result in uneven breathing gas distribution and result in hypoxemia. A sedationist should keep this in mind while increasing the dose of nitrous oxide

3. **Oxygen requirement**: The oxygen need of a child is twice that of an adult resulting from a higher metabolic rate. So, a child is more prone to develop hypoxemia.

	Oxygen consumption	Functional residual capacity
5 kg	9 ml/kg x min	10 ml/kg
10 kg	7 ml/kg x min	15 ml/kg
20 kg	6 ml/kg x min	30 ml/kg
Adults	3.5 ml/kg x min	35ml/kg

Table 7.3 Oxygen consumption and functional residual capacity according to weight

4. **Cardiovascular parameters are different for children**

- Compared to an adult, the heartbeat is quicker, and the blood pressure is lower.
- Bradycardia, reduced cardiac output, and hypotension are more likely to affect children. In contrast to adults, children's blood

pressure is mostly determined by heart rate. Children do not have as well-developed compensating measures to keep blood pressure at a healthy level when the cardiac rate is slowed. As a result, a drop-in heart rate also results in a drop in blood pressure and tissue oxygenation. When administering medications to paediatric age groups that slow the heart rate, this idea must be fully understood.

- In children, a drug's effect and length of action are significantly more variable. Particularly in children who are fat, retention for more lipophilic drugs may be prolonged. Drug metabolism may increase in some patient types. Children may experience faster medication onset from intramuscular drug administration due to improved peripheral perfusion.[3]

One concludes that the dose is more than just applying a formula to derive a proportion of a substance's mature dosage because of the anatomical and physiological variations between kids at various age levels and grown-ups. Children's medication dosages should carefully be customised for each patient in accordance with predetermined standards.

• • •

References

1. Hall JE, Hall ME. Guyton and Hall textbook of medical physiology e-Book. Elsevier Health Sciences; 2020 Jun 13.
2. Malamed SF. Sedation-e-book: a guide to patient management. Elsevier Health Sciences; 2017 May 3.
3. McDonald RE, Avery DR, Dean JA. Dentistry for the child and adolescent 8th edition, Mosby, St. Louis. 2004;288:307-8.
4. From Brodsky L. Modern assessment of tonsils and adenoids. Pediatr Clin North Am 1989;36:1551-1569; and Cote CJ, et al. A practice of Anesthesia for Infants and Children. Philadelphia,

WB Saunders, 1993:313-314.

5. Adewale L. Anatomy and assessment of the pediatric airway. Pediatric Anesthesia. 2009 Jul;19:1-8.

CHAPTER VIII

Nitrous Oxide Sedation Equipment

Practitioners frequently conclude that the nitrous oxide machine is a sophisticated arsenal. However, the fundamental apparatus, which is rather easy to understand, can be generically categorised as a source of gases and a device for their delivery.

The sedation unit is a modified general anaesthesia machine that is made to only provide two gases (nitrous oxide and oxygen), as opposed to the GA machine's ability to supply a number of inhalation agents.

Classification of N_2O Sedation Equipment[1,2]

A.Based on the mobility of the equipment[2]

Nitrous oxide delivery system	
Portable	Centralized
• Flowmeter—digital/analog (mounted on trolley) • Cylinders mounted on yoke with pressure gauges and regulators • Breathing circuit • Scavenging pump/passive scavenging	• Cylinders • Manifold with pressure gauges and regulators • Gas outlets • Flowmeter assembly—digital or analog (trolley/cupboard/wall mounted) • Breathing circuit • Scavenging pump/passive scavenging (**A certified Medical Gas Plumber *must* be contracted for installation of a centralized Gas "Copper Piping" system**)

Table 8.1 Broad categorization of nitrous oxide delivery system.[2]

B. Based on the flow of the unit

1. **Demand Flow Units**

These devices adjust the rate and volume of given gases in accordance with the patient's breathing needs rather than continually supplying gases to the patient. In hospitals and ambulatory settings, a demand flow unit is known as Nitronox, or Entonox TM (BOC Group, England) is employed.

Advantage –

- Lower utilisation of compressed gas volume.

Disadvantages –

- Nowhere in the machine is the volume flow of anaesthetic gases per minute displayed or registered.
- The mixer valve is inaccurate.
- Fatalities have occurred due to the misunderstanding of the use of demand flow units

2. **Continuous Flow Units**

- Regardless of the breathing pattern, these devices have flowmeters and are characterized by a constant flow of gases. It is the most popular style of inhaling unit.
- A disadvantage is that continuous flow devices' accuracy and safety more than make up for the higher amount of gas they utilize over time.[1]

The same fundamental elements can be found in all inhalation sedation devices which are-

1. Compressed Gas Cylinders
2. Reducing Valves
3. Pressure gauges
4. Flowmeters
5. Reservoir bags
6. Conducting tubing

7. Full face mask/ nasal hood/ Nasal cannula[2,4]

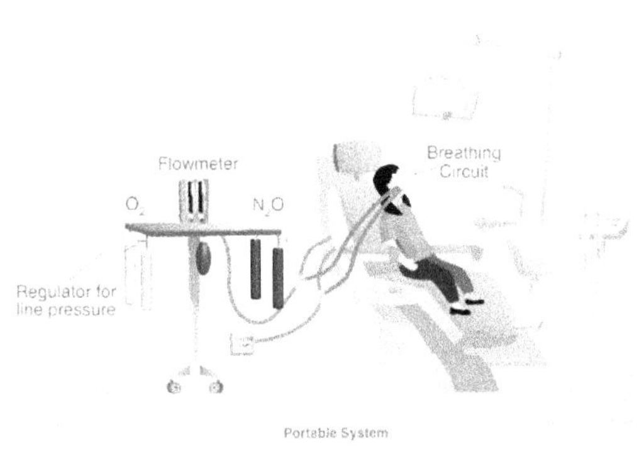

Fig. 8.1 Parts of portable nitrous oxide delivery system.[2]

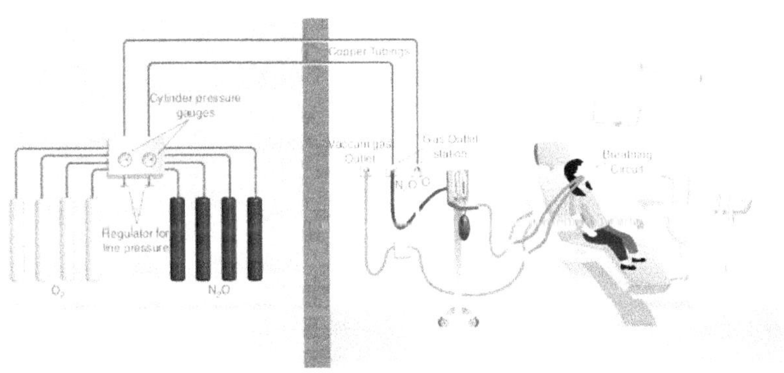

Fig. 8.2 Parts of centralized system of nitrous oxide delivery.[2]

1. Compressed Gas Cylinders: According to the Hazardous Materials Regulations of the U.S. Department of Transportation (DOT), compressed gases are those that are delivered at a pressure greater than 25 pounds per square inch at 25 degrees Celsius. Both health-related and non-health-related occupations employ these gases (e.g., construction, automobiles etc). The DOT has established guidelines that must be followed when transporting and handling these cylinders because to the potential danger. Steel 3/ 8 inch thick should be used to make these cylinders. Cylinders ought to be built to withstand 1.66 times the typical pressure. Additionally, a uniform colour coding for these gas cylinders has been established by the medical community, the American Hospital Association, and the American Society of Anaesthesiology. The valves or opening of these cylinders should not be exposed to any type of oil, grease, or lubricant. They ought to be kept vertically stacked. When not in use, all of the cylinder valves should be closed. Before connecting cylinders to the sedation unit, they should be "cracked." It entails slightly opening the cylinder to let some gas escape, carrying dust and other debris with it. There are different sizes of compressed gas cylinders produced, with "A" being the smallest and "HH" being the largest.[2,4,5]

Colour coding and physical properties of gases in cylinders

	Oxygen	Nitrous oxide	Entonox	Air	Carbon dioxide
Physical state in cylinder	Gas	Liquid	Gas	Gas	Liquid
Critical temperature (°C)	-118	36.5	-7 (pseudocritical temperature)	-141	31
Pressure at 15°C (KPa)	13,700	4400	13,700	13,700	5000
Critical pressure (KPa)	5079	7260	-	3773	7380
Boiling point at 1 atmosphere (°C)	-183	-89	-	-194	-79
ISO colour coding					
Body	Black	Blue	Blue	Black	Grey
Shoulder	White	Blue	White/Blue	White/black	Grey

Table 8.2 Colour coding and physical properties of gases in cylinders[8]

The Oxygen Cylinder and Contents: A pressurized gas canister contains O_2 in a gaseous state and is color-coded white outside of the United States. Depending on the size of the cylinder, the pressure varies from 1900 psi to 2200 psi (G or H). 660L of gas will be produced by a full O_2 gas cylinder. Since oxygen is only present in gaseous form, the pressure gauge merely displays the cylinder's actual contents. As oxygen exits, the pressure will be shown to decrease as a result.

The Contents of the Nitrous Oxide Cylinder: The cylinders contain liquid and gaseous N_2O in varying amounts. 90 to 95 per cent of it is liquid. The N_2O vapour is present above the tank's liquid. There is a 750-psi gas pressure. Blue color-coding is used for these gas cylinders. 1600L of gas will be produced by a full N_2O cylinder. The pressure gauge will display "full" if there is liquid N_2O in the cylinder because of its presence. The gaseous vapour above the liquid is under 750 psi of pressure. New gas is created from the liquid underneath as this gas leaves. When there is no longer any liquid to turn into gas, this process continues, and the pressure gauge then drops in accordance with the pressure of the remaining vapour (like in the oxygen cylinders).

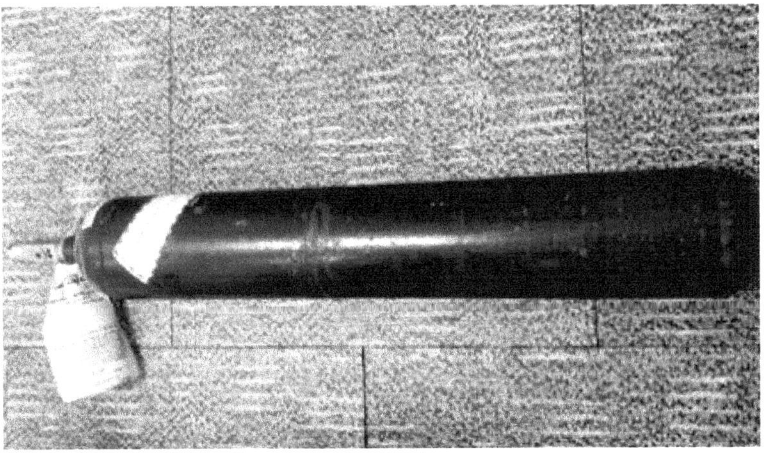

Fig. 8.3 Nitrous oxide cylinder made of steel.[2]

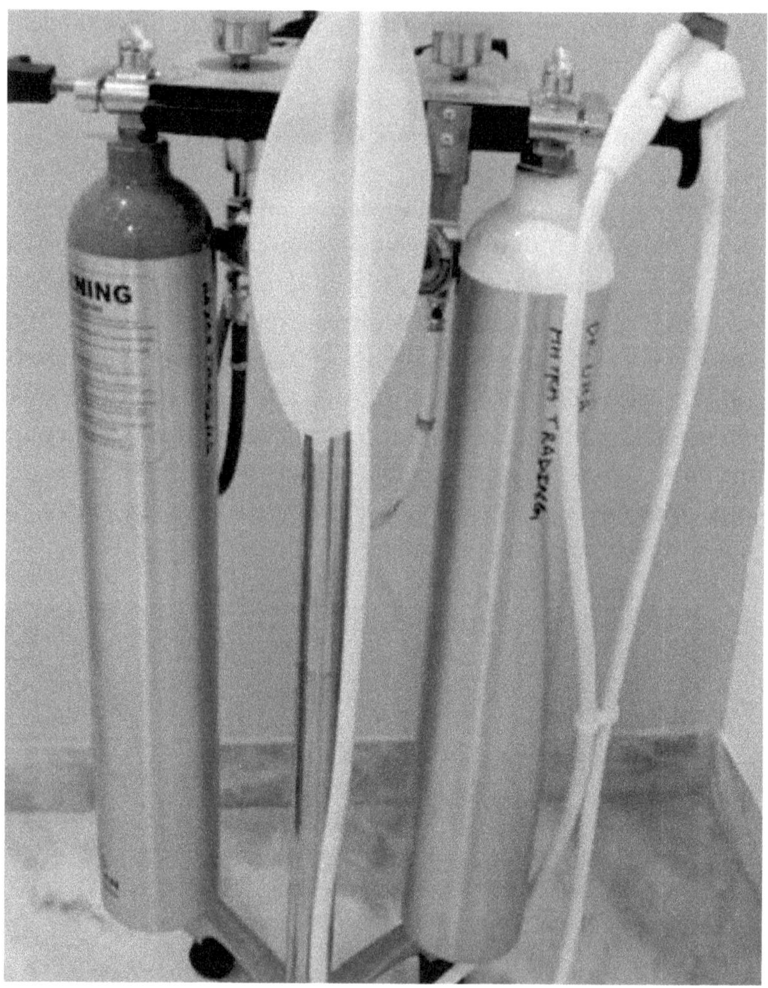

Fig. 8.4 Aluminium cylinders of nitrous oxide and oxygen.[2]

2. Regulators: They are positioned between the compressed gas cylinders and the flowmeter and are also known as reduction valves. The regulator's primary job is to lower the cylinder's high-pressure gases so that both the individual and the sedation device can be used safely. The likelihood of the machine being harmed by high-pressure gases is reduced by maintaining a steady, relatively low pressure inside the N_2O unit's body. The recompression of gases within the reducing valves results in a significant temperature increase of between 815°C and 1100°C. Any oil, grease, or lubricant in contact with this rising temperature will catch fire and explode.[2,4,6]

3. Manifolds for Central System: The manifold connects several gas cylinders. For example, the number of hoses present on a single manifold (12 per se) can be the number of cylinders attached to the hose. This setup allows for multiple treatment areas all connected to a single-cylinder system.

4. Yoke for Portable System: The yoke stand serves as the equipment's supporting structure and backbone in a portable gas supply system. On wheels, this item is quite portable and may be moved from one location to another. Some of the yolk stands in this delivery unit can store two tanks, while others can hold four tanks. The metal framework next to the stand, to which the cylinders are fastened, is known as the yoke. The cylinder must fit into and be properly attached to the unit according to a certain attachment arrangement. The yoke to which the cylinder is attached is punctured by specially placed metal pins. Metal pins underneath the nipple's collar are positioned so that they can only take one particular kind of compressed gas. In the Portable inhalation unit, the high–pressure system is that portion that transfers gases from the cylinders entering the reduction valve through into the yoke; from here to the patient is the low–pressure system. On the boxlike portion of the unit regulators switches, knobs, etc are found on the portable systems.[2,4,6]

5. Flowmeters: Various gases are sent into the equipment's rear by low-pressure piping from the reduction valves. The gases are then routed to the flowmeters, allowing the administration to precisely provide either gas to the individual in the desired volume. Atop the yoke assembly is the calibrated equipment known as the flow metre. The flow metre is traversed by gas leaving the cylinder. The volume of gas being given to the patient is shown by the flowmeter. The flow of gas is measured by the flow metre as it enters various portions and is ultimately visible in the gas pipes on the exterior of the device.

Only the gases that will pass through a flowmeter will determine its calibration. (N_2O or O_2). At 25°C and 76 cm Hg, gas streams are adjusted to be read. Gas flow is measured in litres per minute according to the calibration on the flowmeter. For each flowmeter, a tiny needle valve allows for flow adjustments. The gas flow regulating knobs have both touch and colour coding. The flowmeter uses the rotameter, ball, and rod inside to estimate the gas flow, respectively. The anaesthetic gases are blended in the mixing chamber as they exit through the apex of their individual flow metres and from this point, a mixture of gases exits the outflow tubing and is carried to the patient.

Among the various advances in the types of equipment, the LED flash-containing ones provide the practitioner with an easy way to make sure that each individual gas component, as well as the relative ratio and volume of flow, are accurate. The electronic digital flow control devices' unsilenced alarm feature (Centurion Mixer and Digital MDM) for oxygen depletion ensures patient safety. (New look at old technique).[2,4,5]

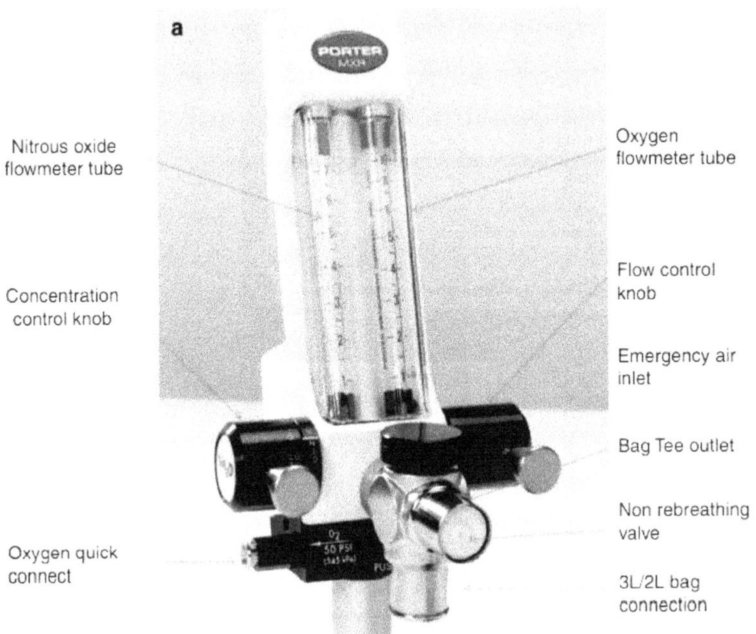

Fig. 8.5 Parts of flowmeter assembly.[2]

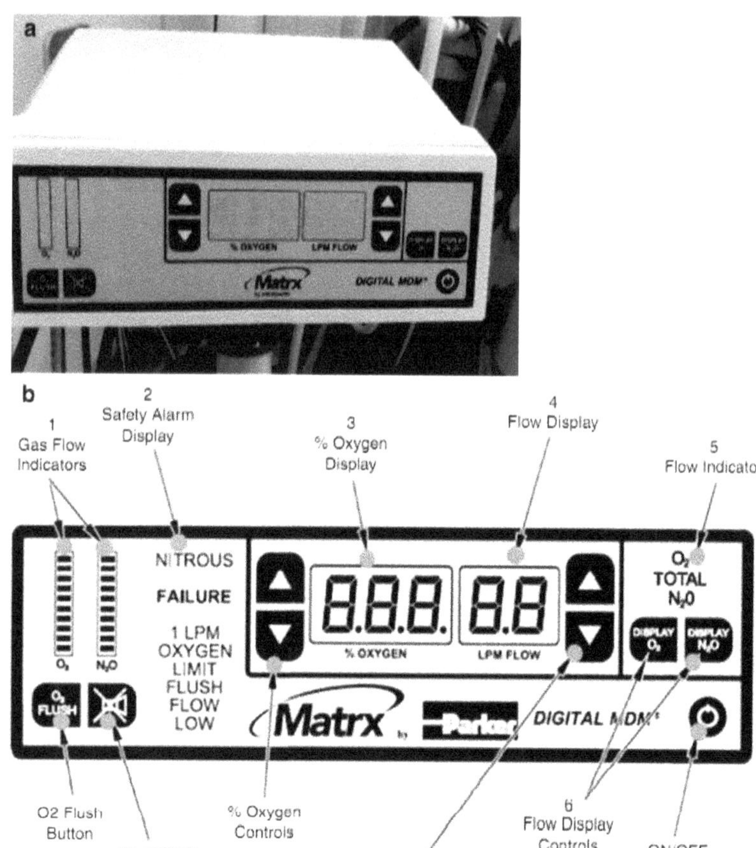

Fig. 8.6 (a) Digital Flowmeter. (b) Parts of Digital Flowmeter. (Courtesy: Porter Inc.)

Rubber Goods: These consist of a Reservoir bag, conducting tubings and the nasal hood.

a. **Reservoir bags**: These bags, which range in size from 1L to 8L and are composed of silicone or rubber, are shaped like bladders. Although lighter bags could be used for young patients, the

3-litre reservoir pouch is most typically used in dentistry. The base of the bag/tee is where the reservoir bag is attached (mixing chamber). It serves the following purposes: it primarily provides a source of additional gas. By keeping an eye on the bag's contraction and relaxation while the patient is sedated, it provides a system for tracking the patient's breathing and ensuring the operator that the patient is inhaling and exhaling gases. The reservoir bag serves as a means of giving the individual positive pressure O_2 in an emergency. The bag is gently pressed, much like a mechanical resuscitation bag, to release its components into the pulmonary tree. Resistance is addressed when a face covering mask with a moderate seal is used in place of a nasal hood to assist airflow.

b. **Conducting Tubes**: The bag/tee and nasal hood are connected by a flexible tube known as the conducting or breathing tube. The tube is corrugated, has a high diameter, and is composed of black latex. The corrugation and big diameter prevent accidental tube kinking and any type of restriction to the movement of gases, respectively. The child's breathing equipment is connected to the corrugated tube by one or two noncorrugated tubes. These have a smaller diameter and come from each side of the head of the dental chair in such a way that the patient remains comfortable.

c. **Breathing Apparatus**: The patient's lips and nose are both covered by the full-face mask. Even though the full-face mask is the best efficient technique to transfer gases, it is problematic for dental treatments since the mouth must be open. But having a full-face mask available in a dental clinic is crucial in an emergency because it allows for speedy oxygen supply. The second form is a **nasal cannula**, which inserts two small, supple plastic hooks into the child's nose. It is typically used to incorporate oxygen for hospitalised patients. With this device, it is impossible to attain an airtight seal, and there is significant gas loss and waste. The **nasal hood** is a piece of equipment made to fit snugly over the child's nose. There are two different kinds;

the conventional one (nosepiece) has one or two tubes inserted into it. The surrounding atmosphere receives the expelled gases. The more sophisticated scavenging nasal hood is the second kind of nasal hood. There are 4 tubes that enter it. The other tubes transport expelled gases away from the procedure area to a secure repository while two tubes provide new gases from the sedation unit. This kind is now required due to growing concern over potential difficulties for the crew. In order to prevent gas from leaking through the sides of the child's nose, the nasal hood is made to fit securely over the nostrils. Nasal hoods are accesible in several sizes to fit appropriately to the size of the nose and different flavours are available for the patient's acceptance. Current models of nasal hoods available are disposable (not sterilizable) or reusable (must be sterilized).[2,4,5,7]

Ingrid Andersson et alin 1989 showed the effectiveness of one of the earliest scavenger hoods called the Anevac-D. The patient acceptance and applicability were judged. It was declared as an excellent scavenger system and exposure levels were found to be within the allowed range by the Swedish Board of Occupational Safety and Health. Since then, many modifications and improvements have been done to better the quality of active scavenging machines which will help in reducing the risk of chronic exposure to the operatory staff.[9]

Another study was done by **Aikaterini et al in 2006** compared the effectiveness of two scavenging nasal hoods which are the newest devices used today i.e. Porter/Brown and Accutron. They concluded that the removal of waste nitrous oxide was more with Brown than with Accutron and found that the ambient level was more with Accutron (101 ppm in the room) than with Brown (10 ppm in the room).[10]

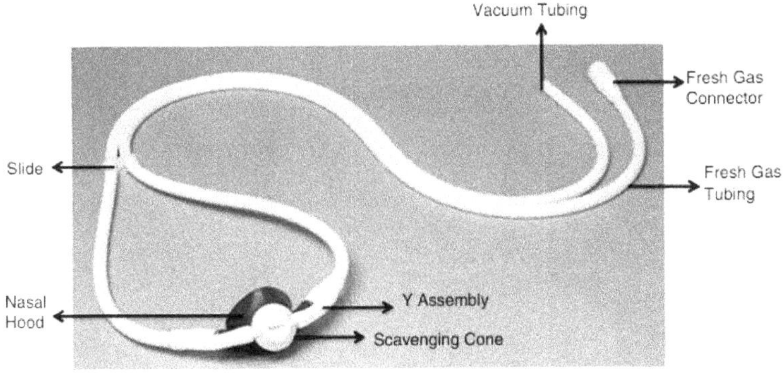

Fig. 8.7 Parts of breathing circuit.[2]

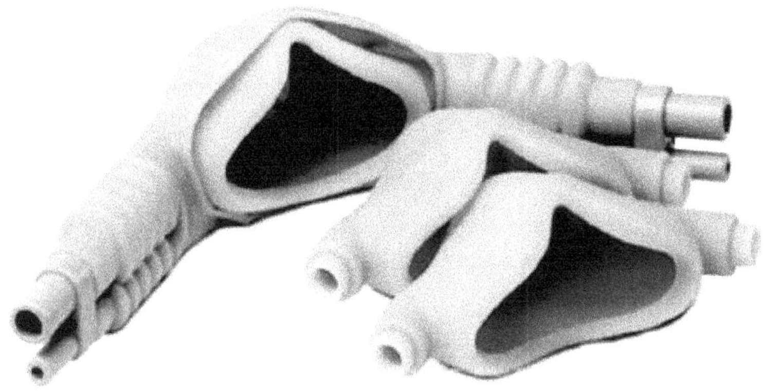

Fig. 8.8 Contoured masks.[2]

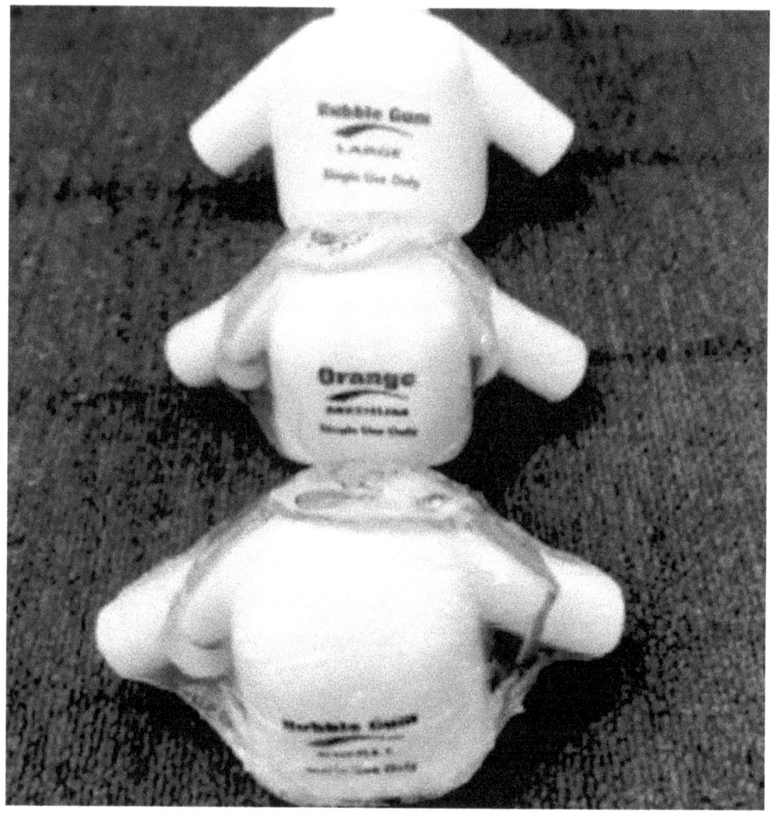

Fig. 8.9 Scented masks of varying sizes.[2]

Safety features of the machine

All inhalation sedation units have incorporated a series of safety features to prevent accidents and emergencies while delivering the gas to a patient. These are-

1. **Pin Index Safety System:** It is comprised of three rows of connectors on the sedation equipment's yoke., each of which is configured differently for each compressed gas, and a corresponding series of holes on the compressed gas cylinders. Consequently, it is not possible to attach an N_2O cylinder to the yoke attachment for O_2 in a practical manner.

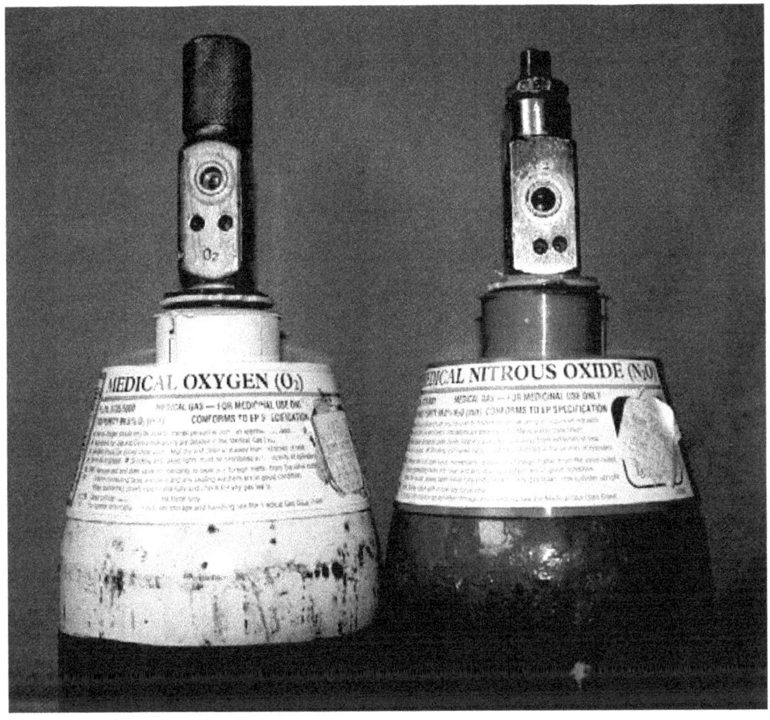

Fig. 8.10 Gas cylinders illustrating the differences in the pin-index between oxygen and nitrous oxide.[11]

2. **Diametric Index Safety System:** It guarantees that the proper medicinal gases are injected into the proper area of the anaesthesia machine. Firstly, the attachment sizes are different (bigger for N_2O and smaller for O_2), and secondly, the threading at the yoke assembly is also different.

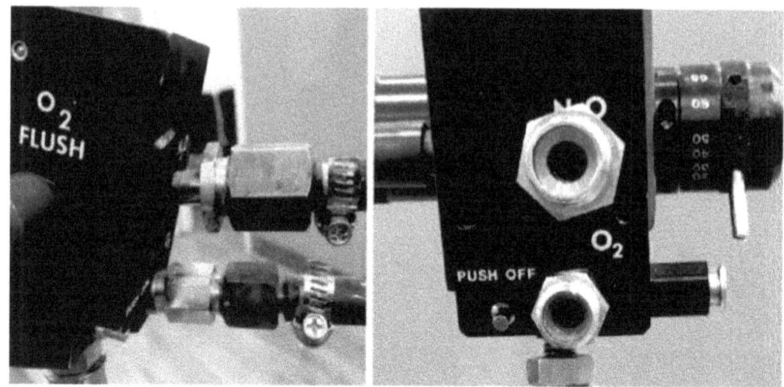

Fig 8.11 DISS on flowmeter assembly showing nitrous oxide with larger diameter (above) and oxygen with a smaller diameter (below).[2]

3. **Minimum Oxygen Litre Flow**: Inhalation devices are created to give a baseline flow of 2.5 or 3 L/min of oxygen once they are switched on. Before the supply of oxygen is begun, the transport of N_2O cannot begin.

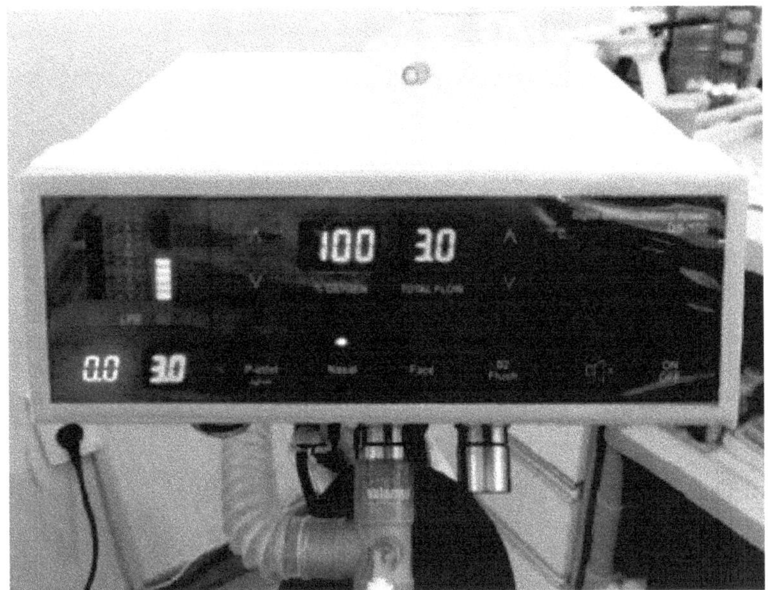

Fig. 8.12 Figure showing minimum oxygen liter flow.[2]

4. **Minimum Oxygen percentage**: The baseline O_2 percentage that may be delivered to a patient is 30% in almost all the sedation units manufactured today. This will prevent 100% nitrous oxide delivery to the patient.
5. **Oxygen Fail-Safe**: The cylinder of oxygen will run out before the cylinder of nitrous oxide in either the portable or central system. 2.5 cylinders of oxygen are needed for every N_2O cylinder. When O_2 runs out, this O_2 fail-safe device prevents the supply of 100% N_2O by stopping the flow of N_2O.

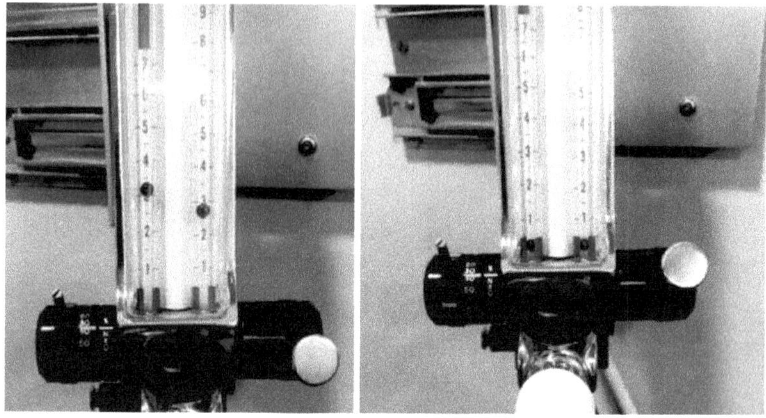

Fig. 8.13 Nitrous oxide flow stops if oxygen flow is interrupted (right).[2]

6. **Emergency Air Inlet**: The emergency air intake, which is above the bag/tee outlet, is kept shut if O_2 or N_2O-O_2 is administered via the sedation unit. The emergency air intake opens when the gas flow stops, allowing the patient to breathe comfortably.

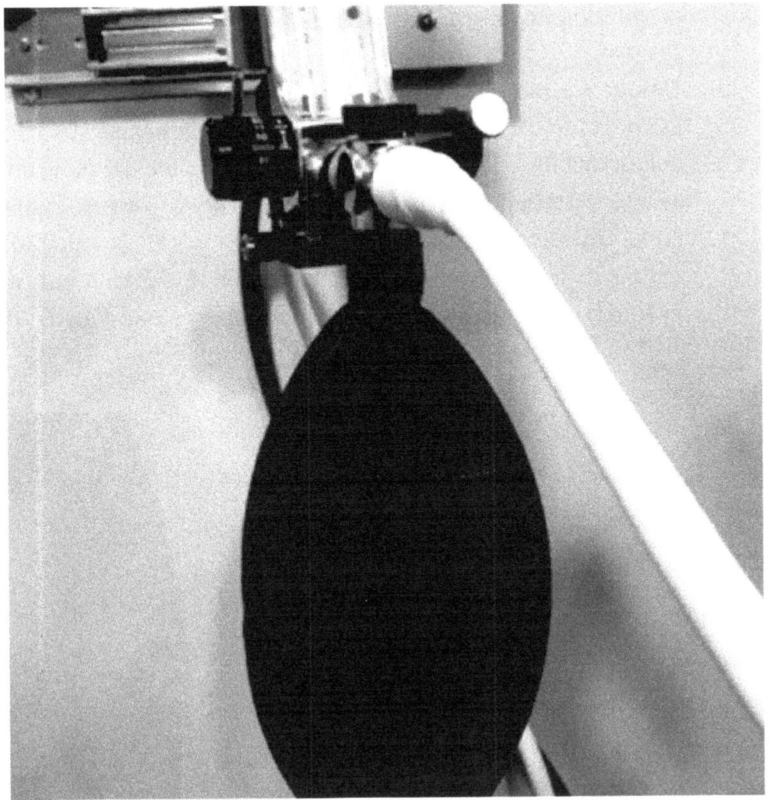

Fig. 8.14 Figure showing deflated reservoir bag. In this situation, emergency air inlet allows inhalation of ambient air.[2]

7. **Alarms**: Recent delivery systems with high-quality performance include audio alarms, digital readouts, and tactile sensitive features.
8. **Oxygen Flush Buttons**: The patient can quickly receive high amounts of O_2 thanks to the O_2 flush button. The equipment automatically stops the N_2O delivery when the O_2 flush button is hit in modern electrical devices, ensuring 100% O_2 delivery. In an emergency, this automation is a clear benefit. The button is conveniently placed in front of the device where it can be seen.

9. **Reservoir Bag**: Because it can be utilised to aid or regulate respiration in times of need, it may be regarded as a safety feature.
10. **Colour Coding**: The non-conductive tubes connecting the gas cylinders to the mixer and the gas cylinders themselves are also colour labelled. The non-conductive tubings are the same colour as the cylinders in terms of colour. While oxygen cylinders come in diverse colours around the world, nitrous oxide cylinders are always blue (e.g., it is green in the USA and white in India). The flowmeter's backdrop is also colour coded.[2,4,6,7]

Fig. 8.15 Figure showing color coding of tubes—blue for nitrous oxide and white for oxygen.[2]

Available inhalation sedation units

There are currently many inhalation sedation machines that can be used in dentistry offices. There are undoubtedly noticeable changes in appearances despite the fact that the underlying mechanism is the same. While some units are constructed of plastic that has been moulded, others feature a veneer of wood. While others are small, some are extremely big. In order to allow clinicians to more thoroughly assess inhalation sedation equipment they are considering buying; the American Dental Association has created an Acceptance Program. The producer must submit their products to the ADA's Council on Scientific Affairs for review to earn a fair grade.

According to a survey done of the American Academy of Pediatric Dentistry members, the most popularly used machine was the **Porter Brown** system. The others that were in use were McKesson, Quantiflex and Accutron. The Matrix MDM system is currently finding its way into the commercial stream of the nitrous oxide sedation machine.A lot of comparison studies have been done regarding the equipment scavenger effectiveness and accuracy of the machines. The two parameters appear to be the most basic way to judge whether a machine is performing efficiently or not.[12]

G.D. Allen and W.M. Goebel conducted a comparative study of 13 sedation machines in use in July 1978. In their study they showed that failure to achieve adequate sedation cannot be blamed on the machines used, however, clinical judgment is the most crucial aspect to assess whether a patient is properly sedated for the required procedure or not. The list of machines tested was

- Dupaco (3)
- Quantiflex R.A. (3)

- Quantiflex M.D.M.
- Dentatron
- Starflite Dentatron
- McKesson Analor III
- Veriflo
- N.C.G. Chemetron
- Sedatron.

Only the Quantiflex had an inaccuracy above 5% (which is the range to begin about any change in sedation level inpatient). The rest of them had an accuracy level well within 5%. The McKesson Analor III had the highest level of accuracy.[13]

Another study by **Jastak and Donaldson** in 1991 showed the comparison of nasal masks tested for scavenging adequacy. The results showed that the McKesson gave the least amount of ambient nitrous oxide in the dental facility.[14]

• • •

References

1. Lowrie L, Weiss AH, Lacombe C. The pediatric sedation unit: a mechanism for pediatric sedation. Pediatrics. 1998 Sep 1;102(3):e30-.
2. Gupta K, Emmanouil D, Sethi A, editors. Nitrous Oxide in Pediatric Dentistry: a clinical handbook. Springer Nature; 2019 Dec 4.
3. Avery DR, McDonald RE. McDonald and avery dentistry for the child and adolescent-E-book. Elsevier Health Sciences; 2010 Apr 8.
4. Clark MS, Brunick AL. Handbook of nitrous oxide and oxygen sedation. Elsevier health sciences; 2008.
5. Malamed SF, Clark MS. Nitrous oxide-oxygen: a new look at a very old technique. CDA. 2003 May 1;31(5):397-404.

6. Marylou Austin R. Nitrous oxide sedation: clinical review & workplace safety. Academy of Dental Learning & OSHA Training, Albany. 2013 Mar.
7. Yee R, Wong D, Chay PL, Wong VY, Chng CK, Hosey MT. Nitrous oxide inhalation sedation in dentistry: An overview of its applications and safety profile. Singapore Dental Journal. 2019 Dec;39(01):11-9.
8. Love-Jones S, Magee P. Medical gases, their storage and delivery. Anaesthesia & intensive care medicine. 2007 Jan 1;8(1):2-6.
9. ANDERSSON-WENCKERT IN, Häggmark S, Johansson G, Lindkvist R, Reiz S. Anevac-D, a new system for close scavenging of anesthetic gases in dental practice. European Journal of Oral Sciences. 1989 Oct;97(5):456-64.
10. Chrysikopoulou A, Matheson P, Milles M, Shey Z, Houpt M. Effectiveness of two nitrous oxide scavenging nasal hoods during routine pediatric dental treatment. Pediatric Dentistry. 2006 May 1;28(3):242-7.
11. Love-Jones S, Magee P. Medical gases, their storage and delivery. Anaesthesia & intensive care medicine. 2007 Jan 1;8(1):2-6.
12. Wilson S. A survey of the American Academy of Pediatric Dentistry membership: nitrous oxide and sedation. Pediatric dentistry. 1996 Jul 1;18:287-93.
13. Goebel WM, Allen GD. Performance of nitrous oxide-0xygen sedation machines. Anesthesia Progress. 1978 Jul;25(4):119.
14. Jastak JT, Donaldson D. Nitrous oxide. Anesthesia Progress. 1991 Jul;38(4-5):142.

CHAPTER IX

Patient Selection And Preperation

For safe and effective sedation that is suited to a particular condition, appropriate patient selection is crucial. Before giving sedatives or anaesthetics to children who are being sedated at any degree, they should be examined. Before beginning treatment, the clinician can accurately assess any potential danger provided by the patient by using it as a recommendation. The following objectives are desired when using this system.[1]

- To assess the patient's psychological tolerance for the pressures associated with the proposed dental treatment.
- To assess whether treatment changes are necessary so the patient can handle the rigours of dental treatment more easily.
- To determine if the application of psycho-sedation is appropriate.
- To determine which sedation approach is best for the patient.
- To ascertain whether any of the drugs that will be administered have any contraindications.

The physical evaluation of the youngster is the initial objective. This consists of three parts.[1]

1. **Medical history questionnaire**: In clinical practise, an ethical and practical obligation is a medical history form. Additionally, it offers important details on the patient's condition. There are numerous medical history forms that come in both short and long form. The University of South California (USC) School of Dentistry's medical history form combines both short and lengthy forms.[1] Medical history should be updated at a minimum of every 6 months.[2] Most common cause of morbidity and mortality associated with pediatric sedation involve airway or

respiratory complications seen in upper respiratory tract infection or common cold.[3] Behaviour evaluation during initial examination is also important to estimate child's cooperation ability. Numerous classification system has been developed that are Wright's (Cooperative, lacking in cooperative ability, potentially cooperative) and Frankl's behaviour rating scale divides into four category (rating 1- definitely negative, 2- negative 3- positive 4- definitely positive).[3]

Child's Name: ______ Date of Birth: ______ Age ______ Date: ______
Address: ______ Telephone: ( ) ______
Physician's name (Medical Doctor): ______ Telephone: ( ) ______

Please circle the appropriate answer

1. Does your child have a health problem? YES NO
2. Was your child a patient in a hospital? YES NO
3. Date of last physical exam: ______
4. Is your child now under medical care? YES NO
5. Is your child taking medication now? YES NO
   If so, for what? ______
6. Has your child ever had a serious illness or operation? YES NO
7. If so, explain: ______
8. Does your child have (or ever had) any of the following diseases?
   - a. Rheumatic fever or rheumatic heart disease YES NO
   - b. Congenital heart disease YES NO
   - c. Cardiovascular disease (heart trouble, heart attack, coronary insufficiency, coronary occlusion, high blood pressure, arteriosclerosis, stroke) YES NO
   - d. Allergy? Food □, Medicine □, Other □ YES NO
   - e. Asthma □ Hay Fever □ YES NO
   - f. Hives or a skin rash YES NO
   - g. Fainting spells or seizures YES NO
   - h. Hepatitis, jaundice or liver disease YES NO
   - i. Diabetes YES NO
   - j. Inflammatory rheumatism (painful or swollen joints) YES NO
   - k. Arthritis YES NO
   - l. Stomach ulcers YES NO
   - m. Kidney trouble YES NO
   - n. Tuberculosis (TB) YES NO
   - o. Persistent cough or cough up blood YES NO
   - p. Veneral disease YES NO
   - q. Epilepsy YES NO
   - r. Sickle Cell disease YES NO
   - s. Thyroid disease YES NO
   - t. AIDS YES NO
   - u. Emphysema YES NO
   - v. Psychiatric treatment YES NO
   - w. Cleft lip/palate YES NO
   - x. Cerebral palsy YES NO
   - y. Mental retardation YES NO
   - z. Hearing disability YES NO
   - aa. Developmental disability YES NO
     If yes, explain: ______
   - bb. Was your child premature? YES NO
     If yes, how many weeks ______
   - cc. Other: ______
9. Does your child have to urinate (pass water) more than six times a day? YES NO
10. Is your child thirsty much of the time? YES NO
11. Has your child had abnormal bleeding associated with previous surgery, extractions or accidents? YES NO
12. Does he/she bruise easily? YES NO
13. Has he/she ever required a blood transfusion? YES NO
14. Does he/she have any blood disorders such as anemia, etc? YES NO
15. Has he/she ever had surgery, x-ray or chemotherapy for a tumor, growth, or other condition? YES NO
16. Does your child have a disability that prevents treatment in a dental office? YES NO
17. Is he/she taking any of the following?
   - a. Antibiotics or sulfa drugs YES NO
   - b. Anticoagulants (blood thinners) YES NO
   - c. Medicine for high blood pressure YES NO
   - d. Cortisone or steroids YES NO
   - e. Tranquilizers YES NO
   - f. Aspirin YES NO
   - g. Dilantin or other anticonvulsant YES NO
   - h. Insulin, tolbutamide, Orinase, or similar drug YES NO
   - i. Any other? ______
18. Is he/she allergic to, or has he/she ever reacted adversely to, any of the following?
   - a. Local anesthetics YES NO
   - b. Penicillin or other antibiotics YES NO
   - c. Sulfa drugs YES NO
   - d. Barbituates, sedatives, or sleeping pills YES NO
   - e. Aspirin YES NO
   - f. Any other? ______
19. Has he/she any serious trouble associated with any previous dental treatment? YES NO
    If so, please explain: ______
20. Has your child been in any situation which could expose him/her to x-rays or other ionizing radiators? YES NO
21. Last date of dental examination: ______
22. Has he/she ever had orthodontic treatment (worn braces)? YES NO
23. Has he/she ever been treated for any gum diseases (gingivitis, periodontitis, trench mouth, pyorrhea)? YES NO
24. Does his/her gums bleed when brushing teeth? YES NO
25. Does he/she grind or clench teeth? YES NO
26. Has he/she often had toothaches? YES NO
27. Has he/she had frequent sores in his/her mouth? YES NO
28. Has he/she had any injuries to his/her mouth or jaws? YES NO
    If yes, explain ______
29. Does he/she have any sores or swellings of his/her mouth or jaws? YES NO
30. Have you been satisfied with your child's previous dental care? YES NO

ADOLESCENT WOMEN

31. Are you pregnant now, or think you may be? YES NO
32. Do you anticipate becoming pregnant? YES NO
33. Are you taking the pill? YES NO

To the best of my knowledge, all of the preceding answers are true and correct. If my child ever has a change in his/her health or his/her medicines change, I will inform the doctor at the next appointment without fail.

Parent's Signature: ______ Date ______

MEDICAL HISTORY/PHYSICAL EXAMINATION REVIEW

Date	Addition	Student/Faculty Signatures

Fig. 9.1 Pediatric medical history questionnaire.[14]

2. **Dialogue history**: The severity of these illnesses and any potential risks during planned therapy are evaluated by the clinician after the individual's information has been gathered. The discourse history process is what causes this.[1]

3. **Physical examination**: Additional sources of the data needed to assess the patient's physical condition.[1] These elements are included in this:

a. Monitoring of vital signs-

i) Blood pressure- Younger patients have lower normal ranges than adults. It ranges from 80 +16/ 46 + 16 mm Hg in new-borns to 118 +19/ 60 + 10 mm Hg in 14-year-olds.

AGES	MEAN SYSTOLIC ±2 SD	MEAN DIASTOLIC ±2 SD
Newborn	80 ± 16	46 ± 16
6 mo-1 yr	89 ± 29	60 ± 10*
1 yr	96 ± 30	66 ± 25*
2 yr	99 ± 25	64 ± 25*
3 yr	100 ±25	67 ± 23*
4 yr	99 ± 20	65 ± 20*
5–6 yr	94 ± 14	55 ± 9
6–7 yr	100 ± 15	56 ± 8
7–8 yr	102 ± 15	56 ± 8
8–9 yr	105 ± 16	57 ± 9
9–10 yr	107 ± 16	57 ± 9
10–11 yr	111 ± 17	58 ± 10
11–12 yr	113 ± 18	59 ± 10
12–13 yr	115 ± 19	59 ± 10
13–14 yr	118 ± 19	60 ± 10

Fig. 9.2 Normal Blood Pressure for Various Ages.[15]

ii) Heart rate (pulse)- The quality of the pulse, the heart's rhythm, and the number of beats per minute should all be considered. It is recommended to monitor heart rate for at least 30 seconds and ideally for a full minute. Its typical range for new-borns is 70 to 170 beats per minute, while for 10-year-olds it is 70 to 110 beats per minute.

Age	Lower Limits of Normal	Average	Upper Limits of Normal
Newborn	70	120	170
1–11 mo	80	120	160
2 yr	80	110	130
4 yr	80	100	120
6 yr	75	100	115
8 yr	70	90	110
10 yr	70	90	110

Fig. 9.3 Average Pulse Rate at Different Ages.[16]

iii) Respiratory rate- Hypoventilation is seen in case of administration of opiods and hyperventilation is seen in case of fever, fear or alkalosis etc. In neonate normally it is 40 per minute and in 12-year-old, it is 16 per minute.

AGE	RATE/MIN
Neonate	40
1 wk	30
1 yr	24
3 yr	22
5 yr	20
8 yr	18
12 yr	16
21 yr	12

Fig. 9.4 Respiratory Rate by Age.[1]

iv) Temperature- On average, the normal intraoral temperature is 37.0°C (98.6°F). The temperature varies throughout the day (0.5°F to 2.0° F), with the morning and late afternoon being the coolest and warmest times. It is increased by fever, gum disease, need for rapid care, extraction, etc. Avoid administering CNS depressants in this situation.

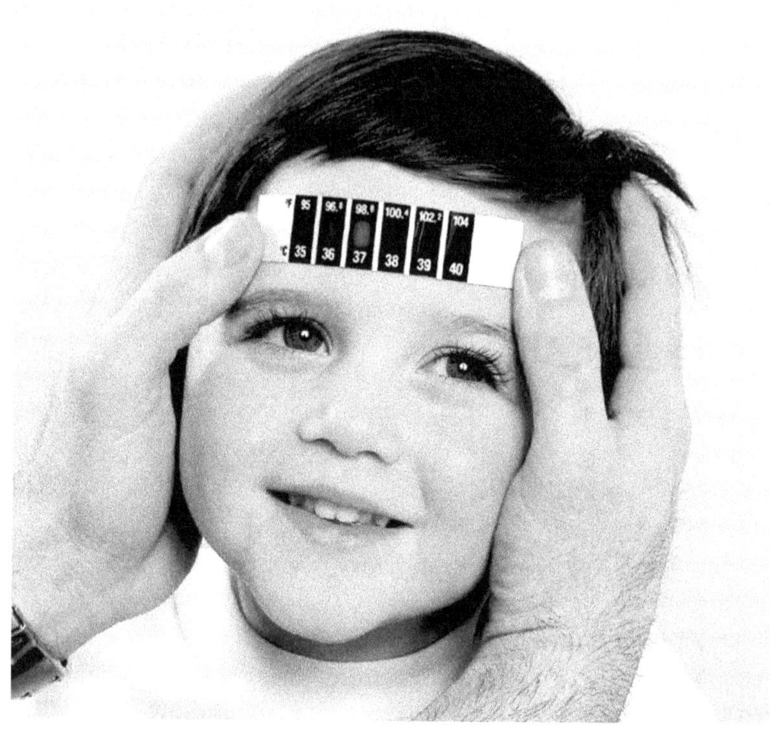

Fig. 9.5 Forehead thermometers are effective when the patient's behavior will not permit use of an oral thermometer. (From Gerdin J: Health careers today, ed 7, St Louis, 2007, Mosby.)

v) Height and weight- It plays a significant role in deciding how much medicine to give kids. The rules of Young and Clark are helpful in calculating paediatric dose. At this time, dose is measured in body weight with units of mg/kg or mg/lb.[1]

b. Visual inspection of patient- Includes thorough oral examination which is necessary for determining time and course of treatment.[3] Additionally, observing the patient's posture, motions, speech, and skin tone aids in the diagnosis of potentially serious illnesses that may have gone undiagnosed in the past. Other factors include exophthalmos, clubbing of the fingers, and prominent jugular veins.[1]

c. Function test and Laboratory tests- This includes hearing the heart and lungs, having the urine and blood tested, having the eyes examined, having the breath-holding test, having an electrocardiogram, and having the blood chemistries done.[1]

Determination of medical risk

Having completed all components of physical evaluation the patient is categorized according to their estimated risk factor.[4] A classification scheme "Physical status classification system" developed by American Society of Anesthesiologist, 1963.[2]

ASA I: A normal healthy patient.

ASA II: A patient with mild systemic diseases e.g. - extremely phobic patient, allergic to drugs or asthmatic or epileptic patient.

ASA III: A patient with severe systemic diseases e.g. - patient with COPDs and less controlled medical condition.

ASA IV: A patient with severe systemic disease that is a constant threat to life e.g. - uncontrolled medical condition.

ASA V: A moribund patient who is not expected to survive without the operation e.g. patient with end stage cancer, lung or renal disorders etc.

ASA VI: A declared brain - dead patient whose organs are being removed for donor purpose.

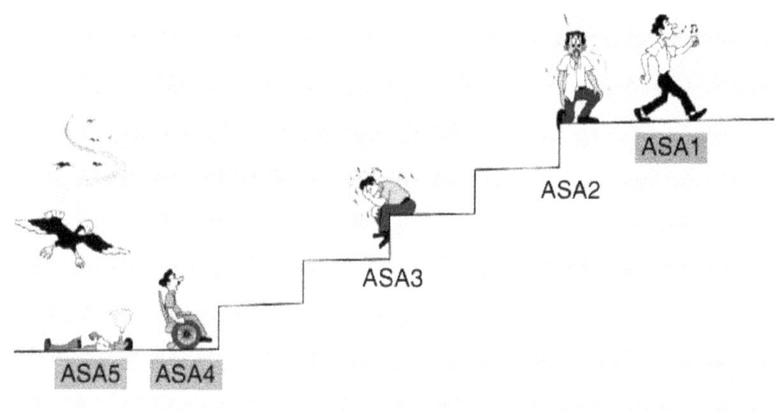

Fig. 9.6 ASA classification.[1]

The patient should fast in accordance with the ASA preprocedural fasting recommendations before receiving nonurgent or emergent procedural sedation. Like clear liquids after two hours of fasting, breast milk after four hours, and light solids after six hours. Considering this evaluation, the choices are-

1. To postpone the procedure.
2. To utilise a milder level of sedation.
3. To use general anaesthesia following rapid sequence end tracheal intubation to secure the airway.

Indications of N_2O-O_2 inhalation sedation[5,6,7]

The management of afraid and nervous youngsters, the management of medically fragile individuals, and the management of gagging are the reasons to employ inhalation sedation. Although many dental operations are typically thought of as harmless or even non-threatening, some patients may find them to be quite upsetting. Many of these processes can use N_2O-O_2 relatively easily.

1. In the management of the fearful or anxious, yet cooperative patients.

The management of dental experience-related phobia and anxiety is the major indication for the use of N_2O-O_2 inhalation sedation in pediatric dentistry. Pediatric dentistry patients that are compliant will display a spectrum of actions and feelings. Some individuals may almost plead for treatment by running into the treatment area, jumping into the chair, and opening their mouths. Others will cautiously enter the treatment area, clutching their family's leg and holding back cries. Even though they are extremely anxious, they will cooperate up until they feel the slightest inconvenience, at which point the floodgates will erupt. This is the ideal circumstance for nitrous oxide/oxygen anxiolysis. Nitrous oxide/oxygen analgesia/anxiolysis can stop a conduct defect if given prior to a potentially unpleasant procedure being done. But the dentist shouldn't believe that putting a nitrous oxide respirator mask on a fearful child will solve all of their difficulties.

2. The patient with a strong gag reflex.

The most fundamental dental therapies- clinical evaluation, radiographic investigation, preventive and fluoride therapy, sealants, and restorative dentistry—can be complicated by a strong gag reflex. Physiological, psychological, and genetic factors are thought to be the causes of a powerful gag reflex. The dentist can use nitrous oxide's ability to reduce gag reflexes if other methods of diversion are unsuccessful. Nitrous oxide does not affect the cough reflex, which means the danger of aspirating unwanted objects while receiving therapy is not increased even though it lessens or negates the gag reaction.[8]

3. The patient that is fearful of specific procedures.

Patients (including children and adults) that the dentist sees are agreeable and tolerant of the dental experience, except for procedures like the "needle or shot" or the drill. The pain and anxiety associated with performing these procedures can be lessened or eliminated because to nitrous oxide's analgesic and anxiolytic qualities. Nitrous oxide can help patients who are uncomfortable with local anaesthetic undergo slightly uncomfortable operations (periodontal scaling, curettage, and modest restorative treatment) without the need for local anaesthetic by raising the patient's pain threshold. The analgesic and anxiolytic qualities of nitrous oxide can assist the patient tolerate the discomfort and psychological trauma of the "shot" or "drill" for those procedures when the use of local anaesthesia cannot be evaded.[8]

4. Certain patients with health care needs and in medically compromised patients

Recent years have seen a rise in the usage of N_2O-O_2 sedation in the care of medically compromised patients.[6]

a) In Cardiovascular Disease.

One of the most effective ways to reduce risk during dental care is to use N_2O-O_2 in patients with cardiovascular disease. An oxygen deficit in the myocardium is one component that is anticipated to cause an aggravation of clinical signs and symptoms in all severe cardiovascular disease states. The risk to the child during dental treatment will reduce with any sedation approach that lowers myocardial O_2 need. N_2O-O_2 inhalation sedation provides various benefits over other sedative methods, including a reduction in anxiety, an increase in the pain reaction threshold, and the provision of at least 30% (but more typically 50% to 70%) of O_2 to the heart and the entire body. With N_2O-O_2 sedation, the patient gets more oxygen than they would from atmospheric air (21 percent).

b) Respiratory Disease.

N_2O can be given relatively safely to asthmatic individuals. Since anaesthetic gases irritate the respiratory mucosa and could trigger an abrupt bout of bronchospasm in asthmatic individuals, many anaesthetic gases are contraindicated. Due to N_2O's non-irritating nature, asthma symptoms are not aggravated. However, due to its euphoric condition, N_2O-O_2 provides a quite secure and successful approach of sedation in these individuals. Sedation is commonly necessary in asthmatic patients since it is possible for increased stress to trigger an abrupt exacerbation of their asthma.

c) Hepatic Disease.

Many medications go through biotransformation in the liver, and when there is significant hepatic dysfunction, this process is hindered. This could lead to increased plasma levels, which could then boost the drug's effect and prolong its therapeutic action. N_2O, however, does not experience biotransformation anywhere in the body and can be employed in patients with hepatic dysfunction with a high chance of success.

d) Epilepsy and Seizure Disorders.

Hypoxic circumstances, elevated stress levels, and anxiety are more likely to cause seizure activity in patients with chronic epilepsy. N_2O can be given to these patients if hypoxia is avoided because it is not an epileptogenic substance and does not raise the likelihood that seizures will occur. The use of N_2O-O_2 inhalation sedation is not prohibited in cases of epilepsy.

e) Attention deficit disorder (ADD) and attention deficit hyperactivity disorder (ADHD).

A study conducted in Texas in 2007 by Carolyn A. et al showed that practitioners believed the incidence of attention deficit disorder in increasing and are aware of the pharmacological means of managing their behaviour. 75% of the respondents in the study preferred the use of Nitrous oxide – oxygen alone whereas, other majority preferred using nitrous oxide – oxygen inhalation along with other oral/IV agents.[9]

f) A patient for whom profound local anaesthesia cannot be obtained.

Local anaesthetic occasionally fails to work. The individual can exhibit a poor pain tolerance or there might be an acute infectious disease present. The patient's pain tolerance is increased by the analgesic effects of nitrous oxide. Giving nitrous oxide before injection may enable the paediatric dentist to give a more pleasant injection in addition to helping with pain control during a difficult treatment.

g) A cooperative child undergoing a lengthy dental procedure.

Younger kids might not be able to sit still for long amounts of time. In addition to altering one's perspective of time, nitrous oxide also enhances the effectiveness of hypnotic suggestion, particularly when using imagery and storytelling.

Contraindications of N_2O-O_2 inhalation sedation

As long as the percentage of O_2 given along with the N_2O is kept above 21%, there are no definite contraindications to using N_2O-O_2 inhalation sedation (O_2 concentration in the atmosphere). There are, however, several relative contraindications to this method. The following conditions make it somewhat inappropriate to utilise N_2O-O_2 inhalation sedation.

1. Chronologically immature child.

Psychologic reassurance is a key component of nitrous oxide/oxygen analgesia/anxiolysis efficacy. The individual needs to be aware of what nitrous oxide is and what to anticipate throughout the operation, especially if they are worried. Only if the patient can comprehend verbal communication will this be possible. Kids (under the age of two) might not be mature enough or able to comprehend the purposes of nitrous oxide/oxygen analgesia/anaesthesia or its results. However, when administered in conjunction with moderate sedation, nitrous oxide/oxygen analgesia/anxiolysis is useful in young children. (The administration of moderate sedation should not be undertaken unless the dentist has had the necessary training.)

2. Behaviourally immature child.

A child that displays inappropriate behaviour for his or her age for reasons other than mental or physical handicap is said to be behaviourally immature. The child could be characterised as overindulged or stubborn using everyday language. This child won't cooperate for dental treatment because they are too afraid or anxious, or because they have a physical or mental impairment; rather, they won't cooperate because they just don't want to. It is not possible to properly deliver nitrous oxide, oxygen analgesia, or anxiolysis to this child until a suitable behaviour modification strategy (voice control, non-verbal communication, positive reward) is utilised to win the child's association.

3. Claustrophobic patients.

Extremely poor effectiveness will be seen in individuals who cannot endure the nasal hood or face mask utilized to administer gaseous substances. The nasal cannula is a possible alternative to the nasal hood in these patients; however, with the increased concern over the inhalation of trace levels of N_2O by paediatric dentist, the use of nasal cannula has fallen out of favour.[10]

4. Patients with severe personality disorders.

Before administering any type of sedation, individuals who are getting psychotropic medications, typically mood-elevating antidepressants, and are getting psychiatric therapy should be thoroughly assessed. Despite the fact that N_2O-O_2 and such psychotropic medicines do not interact negatively, it may be wise to refrain from affecting these people's awareness. It is strongly advised to see a doctor before using any sedative techniques.

5. Upper Respiratory Tract Infections or Other Acute Respiratory Conditions.

A relative adverse reaction to using this approach is any pulmonary condition that prevents the anaesthetic gases from entering the body through the nostrils, since throughout dental treatment procedures, N_2O-O_2 must be taken through the nose. The common cold, acute or chronic sinus issues, chronic mouth breathing, allergies, TB, bronchitis, and cough all depict conditions in which it would be better to avoid using the inhalation sedation method. Effective substitutions can be made with several methods. Of addition to the difficulty in sedating a patient who cannot breathe via their nose, there is a real risk of polluting the inhalation sedation unit's components. Sedation may be given (at a price, of course) to individuals with chronic respiratory conditions or other extremely contagious infections (such as tuberculosis, the human immunodeficiency virus, or AIDS) with their own expendable rubber commodities.

6.Chronic Obstructive Pulmonary Disease (COPD)

Since several COPD individuals have persistently increased CO2 blood concentrations, COPD constitutes a comparative contraindication to inhalation sedation because of the possible impact of doing so. A rise in blood CO2 levels is the typical trigger for respiration in a normal individual; patients with COPD have a weakened or nonexistent capacity to react to this trigger. In its place, the reduced blood O2 concentration in these individuals serves as a respiratory stimulus. They have the involuntary respiratory stimulus eliminated and an O2 enhanced gas mixture that increases blood O2 saturation. Apnea must be monitored in the patient. Chronic apnea does not emerge since the individual can sustain conscious states where active command over respiration is retained.

7. Severe emotional disturbances or drug related dependencies.

When giving nitrous oxide to patients receiving psychiatric or psychologic care, vigilance should be exercised. Antidepressant or psychotropic medications are frequently used to treat patients. Although there is a small chance that prescribed medications will interfere, nitrous oxide may make the underlying disease worse. With a doctor's approval, nitrous oxide can be provided to these people. It is essential that a third party be present in the room during the delivery of nitrous oxide due to the risk of these patients' experiencing hallucinations while under its influence.

8. Middle ear and ophthalmic disturbances.

Nitrous oxide causes an elevation in pressure because it enters the middle ear's stiff, unyielding region. Additionally, the quick removal of nitrous oxide from the gaps at the end of delivery may cause negative pressure. Therefore, nitrous oxide should not be administered to individuals who have recently had surgery or ear, nose, or throat infections. For individuals who have recently had eye surgery, the same is true.

9. Treatment with bleomycin sulphate.

Antineoplastic medication bleomycin sulphate is used to treat squamous cell carcinoma, testicular tumours, and lymphomas. The introduction of nitrous oxide and oxygen may result in an increase in lung fibrosis and illness.

10. Latex sensitivity/allergy.

Latex may be present in some parts of the nasal hoods used to deliver nitrous oxide. Non-latex delivery products can be used in place of latex ones for patients who are sensitive or allergic to it.

11. The patient who does not want N_2O-O_2

N_2O (or any other medication) should never be administered to patients against their consent under any circumstances. This could have unfavourable side effects or legal ramifications.

Documentation

It's time to create a sedation plan that caters to a specific child's needs when the patient assessment is finished. It is crucial to capture the sedative experience meticulously and accurately. An accurate, transparent, ongoing, documented description of what happened before to, during, and following the interaction serves as the best insurance in the event of a negative reaction. Following institutional policy, the many possibilities, risks, and alternatives should be discussed with the child's parent(s) or guardian(s), and informed consent should be acquired and recorded in the patient record.[11] Pre-sedation, intra-sedation, and post-sedation guidelines must be included in the paperwork, and they are as follows:[12.18]

1. Informed consent
2. Instruction and information to responsible person
3. Dietary precautions
4. Personnel
5. Operating facilities and equipment
6. Check list
7. Monitoring
8. Sedation record

9. Discharge criteria
10. General guidelines

Informed Consent

Giving the client, in the case of a child or an incapacitated individual, the custodial parent or legal guardian knowledge regarding the diagnosis and required therapies allows them to make an educated decision regarding the course of action. The American Dental Association's Principles of Ethics state that "the dentist should tell the patient of the recommended therapy, and any acceptable alternatives, in a way that allows the patient to become involved in treatment decisions."[13]

State legislation and judicial decisions set the parameters for informed consent. A New York state court declared in 1914 that every adult person with a healthy mind and appropriate years has the freedom to determine what should be done with his or her own body. State laws and case laws regulate informed consent. In some jurisdictions, verbal agreements must be documented in the medical file, while in others, a documented contract may be required. To assess their degree of compliance, dental professionals should research the relevant state laws. Consent forms should be procedure-specific, use straightforward language, and refrain from making general assertions.

The following information ought to be included on any "informed consent" forms used by practitioners:

- The patient's name and date of birth.
- The patient's name, relationship to the patient, and the legal basis for the permission being given on the patient's behalf.
- A brief explanation of the technique.
- The disclosure of any known risks associated specifically with the proposed treatment.

- Evidence-based or professionally acknowledged alternatives to advised therapy and dangers
- A spot where the custodial parent or legal guardian can signify that all queries have been addressed in full.
- A spot for the dentist, a witness office employee, and the custodial parent or legal guardian to sign.

CONSENT FOR THE USE OF SEDATION OR GENERAL ANESTHESIA
FOR
PEDIATRIC DENTAL TREATMENT

I ____________ as the legally responsible parent or guardian of ____________ give my consent to the use of local anesthetics, sedative drugs, or general anesthetic agents that Dr(s) ____________ may deem necessary on the child's examination chart as previously explained to me and any other procedure deemed necessary or advisable as a cor-ollary to the planned treatment for ____________, except for (if none, so state) ____________

I have been informed and understand that occasionally there are complications of the treatment, drugs, or anesthetic agents, including but not limited to: numbness, infection, swelling, bleeding, discoloration, nausea, vomiting, allergic reactions, brain damage, stroke, or heart at-tack. I further understand and accept that complications may require hospitalization and may even result in death.

Dr(s) ____________ discussed with me, to my satisfaction, these compli-cations. I acknowledge the receipt of and understand the preoperative and postoperative instruc-tions. The treatment and sedation or anesthesia procedures have been explained to me, to my satisfaction, along with possible alternative methods and their advantages and disadvantages, risks, consequences, and probable effectiveness of each, as well as the prognosis if no treatment is provided.

I have read this consent and understand, to my satisfaction, the procedures to be performed and accept the possible risks.

Legally responsible parent or guardian: ____________ Date: ____________

Address: ____________

Witness: ____________

I certify that I explained the above procedures to the parent or guardian before requesting his or her signature.

____________ Date: ____________

Signature of dentist

Fig 9.7 Example of form for informed consent. (Source: Dr. Kenneth C. Troutman)

Instruction and Information to Responsible Person

The responsible person must receive instructions from the clinician verbally and/or in writing. The purpose of the sedation as well as predicted behavioural changes both during and after should be included. To prevent any issues, specific instructions must be given for the safety of new-born transportation as well as a lengthy time of surveillance. All patients must be given a phone number that is available around-the-clock. Limitations on activities and suitable dietary restrictions must be included in the instructions.

Dietary Precautions

Sedatives have the potential to impede reflexes that protect the airways. Pulmonary aspiration, however uncommon, could happen if a youngster regurgitates. Therefore, it is advisable for the clinician to consider the patient's previous dietary intake and hydration intake before sedation. Patients who have experienced recent oral intake, trauma, a drop in consciousness, excessive obesity, or intestinal motility disorder need to be carefully assessed before receiving sedative treatment.[12]

The following should be the dietary recommendations (AAPD Guidelines)

1. Drink clear drinks up to two hours before the treatment, such as water, fruit juices without pulp, fizzy beverages, clear tea, and black coffee.
2. Up to 4 hours before to the surgery, breast milk
3. Up to six hours prior to the surgery, infant formula
4. Up to six hours before the operation, nonhuman milk
5. A little meal two hours prior to the surgery. Toast and light drinks are traditional components of a light supper. Meals that contain fried, fatty, or meat should be avoided because they may take longer for the stomach to empty.

6. It is okay to take regular, required drugs the day of the treatment with a sip of water.

Ingested Material	Minimum Fasting Period, h
Clear liquids: water, fruit juices without pulp, carbonated beverages, clear tea, black coffee	2
Human milk	4
Infant formula	6
Nonhuman milk: because nonhuman milk is similar to solids in gastric emptying time, the amount ingested must be considered when determining an appropriate fasting period.	6
Light meal: a light meal typically consists of toast and clear liquids. Meals that include fried or fatty foods or meat may prolong gastric emptying time. Both the amount and type of foods ingested must be considered when determining an appropriate fasting period.	6

Table 9.1 Appropriate Intake of Food and Liquids Before Elective Sedation.[17]

The reason for these recommendations are two-fold. A potential hazard of sedative therapy is emesis, which can cause aspiration of stomach contents and cause laryngospasm or severe airway blockage. Aspiration pneumonia, a complication of aspiration, may potentially arise later. It at least causes a negative interruption to the daily operations of the office. Second, medication absorption is greatest when the stomach is empty because the majority of sedatives are delivered orally. Additionally, the mother or father or guardian should be informed that they need to stay in the clinic for the sedation procedure. To allow the individual responsible for the child to focus on the child's needs throughout the drive home, the directions for transportation may demand that a second member accommodate the parent.

INSTRUCTIONS TO FOLLOW BEFORE YOUR CHILD'S SEDATION

EATING AND DRINKING

1. No milk or solid foods 6 hours before the sedation appointment
2. Clear liquids such as water, clear juices, gelatin, Popsicles, or broth, may be given up to 3 hours before the appointment
3. Let everyone in the home know the above information, because siblings or others living in the home often unknowingly feed the child

ACTIVITY

1. Plan the child's sleep and awakening times to encourage the usual amount of sleep the day before the sedation appointment.
2. Please arrive on time for your scheduled appointment. This is a long appointment, and you may be here for several hours.
3. The legal guardian must accompany the child to the sedation appointment.
4. A second responsible adult must join you and your child at the time of discharge. This enables one adult to drive the car while the second adult focuses attention on your child after the treatment is completed. The child should be carefully secured in a car seat belt during transportation.
5. Make sure your child uses the restroom before the sedation.

ACTIVITY AFTER THE SEDATION

1. Your child may take a long nap. He/she may sleep from 3 to 8 hours and may be drowsy and irritable for up to 24 hours after sedation. When your child is asleep, you should be able to awaken him/her easily.
2. Your child may be unsteady when walking or crawling and will need support to protect him/her from injury. An Adult must be with the child at all times until the child has returned to his/her usual state of alertness and coordination.
3. Closely supervise any activity for the remainder of the day.

CHANGE IN HEALTH

It is important that you notify the office of the development of a cold, cough, fever, or any illness within 14 days before the sedation appointment. For your child's safety, the sedation may need to be rescheduled.

Fig. 9.8 Example of presedation instructions to the parent or caregiver. (Source: Dr. Kenneth C. Troutman)

• • •

References

1. Malamed SF. Sedation-e-book: a guide to patient management. Elsevier Health Sciences; 2017 May 3.
2. Johnson JD. Conscious Sedation for Dentistry risk management and patient selction. Dent Clin Noth Am. 2002;46:767-80.

3. Silegy T, Jacks ST. Pediatric oral conscious sedation. Journal of the California Dental Association. 2003 May 1;31(5):413-8.
4. Jastak, J. T. and Donaldson, D.: Nitrous oxide. Anesth Prog, 38: 142, 1991
5. Bourgade C, Droz N, Cotillon M, De Groc T, Cojocaru B. The use of nitrous oxide and oxygen in paediatric emergency departments. Soins. Pediatrie, Puericulture. 2016 Jul 1;37(291):39-41.
6. Macpherson JA, Kwasnicki AJ. Conscious sedation. Part one: review of indications and techniques. Dental Nursing. 2011 Feb;7(2):70-5.
7. American academy of Pediatric Dentistry. Guideline on the elective use of conscious sedation, deep sedation and general anaesthesia in pediatric dental patients. Pediatr Dent (Special Issue.); 1998, 20:6; 74 – 80.
8. American Academy of Pediatric Dentistry Reference Manual. Clinical guideline on appropriate use of nitrous oxide for pediatric dental patients. Pediatr Dent 2010/11;32.
9. Kerins CA, McWhorter AG, Seale NS. Pharmacologic behavior management of pediatric dental patients diagnosed with attention deficit disorder/attention deficit hyperactivity disorder. Pediatr Dent. 2007 Nov-Dec;29(6):507-13. PMID: 18254422.
10. Bowen DM. AIDING IN THE ADMINISTRATION OF NITROUS OXIDE-OXYGEN ANALGESIA.
11. Shankar V, Deshpande JK. Procedural sedation in the pediatric patient. Anesthesiol Clin North Am. 2005 Dec;23(4):635-54, viii. doi: 10.1016/j.atc.2005.07.001. PMID: 16310656.
12. American Academy of Pediatrics, American Academy of Pediatric Dentistry. Guidelines for monitoring and management of pediatric patients during and sedation for diagnostic and therapeutic procedures. Pediatrics 2006;118(6):2587-602.
13. American Academy of Pediatric Dentistry. COUNCIL ON CLINICAL AFFAIRS. Guideline on Informed Consent. AAPD Reference Manual. 2010.

14. Malamed SF: Medical emergencies in the dental office, ed 6, St Louis, 2007, Mosby.
15. National High Blood Pressure Education Program Working Group on High Blood Pressure in Children and Adolescents. The fourth report on the diagnosis, evaluation, and treatment of high blood pressure in children and adolescents, Pediatrics 114(2 Suppl 4th Report):555–576, 2004.
16. Kliegman RM, Stanton BF, St. Geme JW, Schor NF, editors: Nelson textbook of pediatrics, ed 20, St Louis, 2016, Elsevier
17. American Society of Anesthesiologists. Practice guidelines for preoperative fasting and the use of pharmacologic agents to reduce the risk of pulmonary aspiration: application to healthy patients undergoing elective procedures. An updated report by the American Society of Anesthesiologists Committee on Standards and Practice Parameters. Available at: https://www.asahq.org/For-Members/Practice-Management/Practice-Parameters.aspx.
18. Cote CJ, Wilson S. Guidelines for monitoring and management of pediatric patients before, during, and after sedation for diagnostic and therapeutic procedures: update 2016. Pediatric dentistry. 2016 Jul 15;38(4):13E-39E.

CHAPTER X

Administration And Monitoring

Operating facilities and equipment

The operating room whereminimal sedation is administered must contain all the amenities and tools previously suggested. The minimum observation device for minimal sedation must be a pulse oximeter, with the possible exemption of level 1 minimal sedation, which is mediated by minor tranquillizers administered orally and/or nitrous oxide and oxygen inhalation sedation at a nitrous oxide concentration of 50% or less. Level 3 prefers capnography.[1] Sphygmomanometers must be provided right away. For level 3, a precordial/pretracheal stethoscope is necessary. The recommended list of tools and supplies is provided below. It may need to be amended depending on the particular clinical condition.[2]

Emergency medications

Albuterol
Amiodarone
Atropine
Calcium chloride or gluconate
Diphenhydramine
Epinephrine (1:1000, 1:10,000)
Flumazenil
Glucose (50%)
Hydrocortisone, dexamethasone, methylprednisolone
Lidocaine
Naloxone
Sodium bicarbonate
Vasopressin

Equipment

Adhesive tape
Alcohol wipes
Endotracheal tubes (2.5-, 3.0-, 3.5-, 4.0-, 4.5-, 5.0-, 5.5-, 6.0-, 6.5-, and 7.0-mm internal diameter)
Face mask (infant, child, small adult)
Gloves
Hypodermic needles
Intraosseous needle
Intravenous catheters (24-, 22-, 20-, and 18-gauge)
Intravenous fluids, including normal saline and lactated ringer solutions
Intravenous tubing and burette drip set
Laryngoscope blades (straight number 1, 2, and 3 and curved number 2, and 3)
Laryngoscope handles
Oral and nasal airways (pediatric sizes)
Oxygen regulator, flow meter, and tubing
Self-inflating or anesthesia bag-valve set (0.5-, 1-, and 2-L sizes)
Source of compressed oxygen (eg, a tank with at least 60 min of supply at high flows or a wall outlet)
Stylets
Suction device (portable or wall outlet)

Suction tubing and canisters
Syringes (1-, 3-, 5-, and 10 mL)
Tourniquets
Yankahuer and soft-tip suction catheters (5-, 8-, 10-, and 12-F)

Monitors

Capnometer (end-tidal CO_2 monitor) with bi-nasal cannula
Defibrillator with pediatric pads or paddles
Monitor with leads & sensors (respiratory rate, heart rate, and ECG)
Pulse oximeter with sensors

Fig. 10.1 Suggested list of equipment and supplies for pediatric sedation.[2]

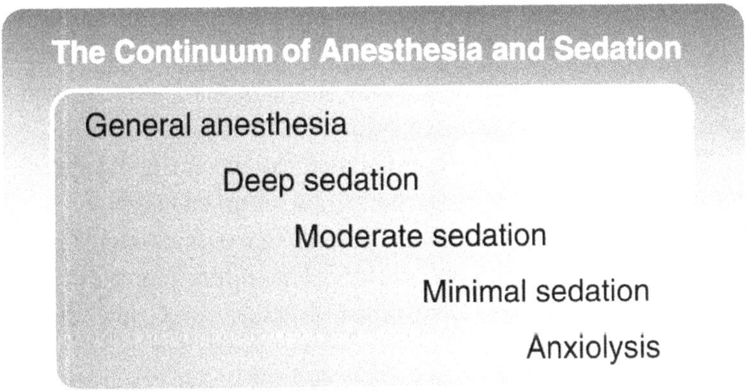

The Continuum of Anesthesia and Sedation

General anesthesia
Deep sedation
Moderate sedation
Minimal sedation
Anxiolysis

Fig. 10.2 Clinical assessment of the level of sedation is usually not as straightforward as the definitions of various levels of anesthesia imply. There is considerable overlap among the levels of sedation, and a patient's level of sedation may easily change throughout the course of a procedure. For this reason, proper vigilance and monitoring are essential for the safe administration of sedation and anesthesia.[9]

Preparation for sedation procedures

Utilizing a methodical approach is a crucial component of the safety net of sedation because it prevents you from forgetting to have a critical medication, piece of equipment, or monitor on hand in the event of an impending emergency. Utilizing an acronym that enables the same setup and checklist for each procedure can help avoid this issue. SOAPME is a well-known abbreviation that can be used to plan and prepare for an operation:[1,3]

S (suction): a functional suction apparatus with suction catheters of the proper size (e.g., Yankauer-type suction)

O (oxygen): a sufficient supply of oxygen and working flowmeters and other equipment to enable its distribution.

A (airway): the proper size airway equipment, including the laryngoscope blades (check and operating), endotracheal tubes, stylets, face mask, bag valve mask, or analogous device, as well as the nasal and oropharyngeal airways (functioning).

P (pharmacy): all the essential medications, including specified antagonists, required to maintain life during an emergency.

M (monitors): a working pulse oximeter with oximeter probes of the proper size and any additional monitors required for the procedure (e.g.,non-invasive blood pressure, end tidal dioxide, ECG, stethoscope).

E (equipment): specialised tools or medications for a certain situation (e.g., defibrillator).

Technique Sequence for administration of nitrous oxide[6,7,8,9]

Step 1

The dentist is required to give a detailed account of the experience if it is the individual's first time using nitrous oxide.

This can help the nervous patient feel less anxious and desensitise (tell, show, do) the patient who is having the procedure for the first time. The patient is informed of what to anticipate in plain language. The patient is presented and given the opportunity to handle the dials, reservoir bag, and, of course, the nasal hood of the delivery unit. Nasal hoods are available in a range of designs, dimensions, forms, and fragrances. Some can be sanitised, while others are disposable. It is advised to fragrance nasal hoods when giving nitrous oxide to children in order to make the experience more pleasant. To prevent the youngster from contaminating the various scents, the nasal hoods are covered in protective plastic. Prior to the restorative session, patients who are exceedingly anxious are provided the nasal hood to go home. This enables them to become even less responsive to the influence of nitrous oxide.

Step 2

In order to approximate the patient's little breathing volume, attach the nasal hood to the hoses and change the oxygen rate of flow. The amount of fresh air an individual breathes in a minute is known as the minute respiratory volume. Tidal volume, or the amount of air in a typical breath, is multiplied by respiratory rate per minute to determine it. The minute respiratory volume of a patient varies with age and body size. The minute respiratory volumes between an adult and a child are not very different even if a grown up may have a larger tidal volume than a toddler due to the latter's higher respiratory rate. Before covering the patient's nose with the nasal hood, it is crucial that gas is flowing. Nothing is more unsettling for a nervous patient than being unable to breathe. The patient cannot breathe without gas flow.

Step 3

To prevent seepage of gas into the environment, the nasal hood is delicately placed and fitted over the individual's nose. For patients who feel uncomfortable about having their nose enveloped with the nasal hood, a version of Step 2 can be tried. Because nitrous oxide is 1.53 times denser than air, when it is released into the aerosphere, it will fall. Prior to seating the nasal hood, nitrous oxide may be added to the oxygen (30 percent / 70 percent concentration) if the patient displays claustrophobia when the nasal hood is placed directly on the nose. Three inches or so are added to the nasal hood's height over the individual's nose. Since nitrous oxide is denser than air, it will fall into the individual's nose where it will be inhaled, presumably causing them to relax. The nasal hood is lowered until it is adequately resting on the patient's nose as the patient unwinds.

Step 4

The reservoir bag is now brought to your attention. If there is a sufficient amount of gas to the individual, the bag will be expanded to half its maximum volume and expand and collapse in rhythm with the individual's respiratory patterns. The bag will burst if the gas flow is too low. The bag will overinflate if there is an excessive gas flow. The right flow rate is set, and it is maintained throughout the process.

Step 5

The individual's ideal nitrous oxide/oxygen concentration is titrated once the optimal flow rate is established. To achieve a concentration of 20% nitrous oxide and 80% oxygen, the titration procedure starts by reducing the oxygen flow and boosting the nitrous oxide supply. For three minutes, this focus is maintained at this level. There shouldn't be much interaction between the individual and the paediatric dentist or assistant. Talking should be kept to a minimum so that nasal breathing can be optimised, and the nitrous oxide/oxygen level is maintained throughout. After three minutes, the dentist asks the patient if they are experiencing any symptoms. Avoid asking leading questions, such as "Do you feel tingling?" Lightheaded? Relaxed? Such inquiries will just increase the nervous patient's anxiety since they will worry that the nitrous oxide is not working properly while they are not experiencing the effects of it. The patient is asked to explain their feelings. If the patient responds that there is no difference, the levels of nitrous oxide and oxygen are changed to 30% nitrous oxide and 70% oxygen.

After three minutes, the procedure is repeated, and the individual is once more asked to explain their feelings. In the event that they have a negative response, the nitrous oxide/oxygen concentration is raised to 40% nitrous oxide and 60% oxygen. Up till the patient displays good symptoms, this procedure may be repeated. However, due to the fool proof and reliant restrictions placed on the distribution unit, the nitrous oxide/oxygen concentration may not go above 70% nitrous oxide and 30% oxygen.

Step 6

Treatment can begin as soon as the patient displays the behaviours categorised under Altered State of Consciousness. To keep the level of nitrous oxide and oxygen constant, nasal breathing should be maximised. This involves speaking with the patient as little as possible and using a rubber barrier to reduce mouth breathing. The patient's facial expression, body position, reaction to questions and usage of the pulse oximeter are used to monitor the patient's degree of awareness. It is important to keep the patient in the Altered State of Consciousness stage and prevent them from slipping into the Loss of Consciousness stage or returning to the Active Alert Consciousness stage. However, frequent changes in the nitrous oxide/oxygen concentration might have the effect of "bouncing" the patient, resulting in headache and nausea following surgery.

Step 7

The nitrous oxide flow is stopped five minutes before the treatment is finished, and the patient is then given 100 percent oxygen. Since nitrous oxide is very soluble and does not easily enter the bloodstream, when the flow is stopped, it is quickly expelled through the alveoli. Throughout this mechanism, nitrogen oxide escapes more quickly than the atmospheric nitrogen that substitutes it, lowering the oxygen blood saturation and diluting the oxygen supply. This syndrome, known as diffusion hypoxia, can cause vertigo (vertigo), headaches, tiredness, and nausea in some individuals after treatment. Before finishing the surgery, administering 100% oxygen for five minutes may help to prevent or lessen these side effects.

Step 8

If the individual does not report any dizziness, headache, nausea, or lethargy after receiving 100% oxygen for five minutes, the nasal hood and gas flow may be stopped. The correct procedure is to remove the nasal hood first, then stop the gas flow. This is the opposite of what happened when gas administration first started. In order to reduce patient anxiety brought on by being unable to inhale gas, the administration started by turning on the gas flow and then covering the patient's nose with the nasal hood. Similarly, we want to allow the individual to breathe ideally until the very end of the treatment.

Signs and symptoms of sedation[2,6,7,8]

Early to ideal sedation: Headaches, tingling, waves of warmth, a vibrational sensation throughout the anatomy, numbness in the hands, feet, and soft tissues of the mouth, euphoria, and lightness or weight in the extremities. Early in the process, there was a slight increase in blood pressure and heart rate, which thereafter returned to normal. There was also smooth breathing, peripheral vasodilation, flushing, and a decrease in muscular tone.

Heavier sedation/ slight oversedation: Increased sensitivity to sound, especially distant sound, clouded vision, increased tiredness, increased sweating, sobbing, laughing, dreaming, and nausea: elevated blood pressure, heart rate, blood flow, respiration, sweating, and potentially lacrimation.

Oversedation: Nausea, persistently closes the mouth, spontaneously begins mouth breathing, sluggish responses, uncoordinated movements, vomiting, loss.

Titration of nitrous oxide

Two basic techniques of administering nitrous oxide gas have been used in the past. One is the constant litre flow technique in which the total litre flow of both gases is kept constant per minute and the other is the titration method. Titration is a method of administering a drug in incremental amounts. Titrating the N_2O dose is the principal technique of administering the gas. It allows only a specific amount of N_2O to be delivered as much required by that patient. It does not allow excess amount to be given to a patient.[4,8] A technique described by Pinkham is the "rapid induction" method in which a large quantity of N_2O i.e. upto 50% is administered initially to patients, especially the extremely anxious or difficult patient to produce immediate calming results. This technique in skilled hands can produce favourable results.

Titration allows for biological variability as many may find a small portion of patients to be either hypo or hyper responders. The initial dose of nitrous oxide should always range between 10 and 20 percent, regardless of the tools or methods employed. Depending on the machine type, either the N_2O knob (or button) can be set to 20% or the O_2 can be set to 80%. Individual gas flows are now automatically adjusted. If the initial flow was 6L/min and the nitrous oxide gas is started, the O_2 flowmeter will automatically reduce while the N_2O flowmeter will show the ball floating at that level. One of the most frequent errors made in this situation is when the operator believes that the flow of N_2O in litres is equivalent to the amount of gas being delivered. It is untrue. It is simple to determine the amount of N_2O being given via:

$$\text{PERCENTAGE OF } N_2O = \frac{\text{Litre/minute } N_2O}{\text{Litre/minute } O_2 + \text{Litre/minute } N_2O}$$

$$\text{PERCENTAGE OF } O_2 = \frac{\text{Litre/minute } O_2}{\text{Litre/minute } O_2 + \text{Litre/minute } N_2O}$$

Once the desired amount of drowsiness is reached, gradually increase the nitrous oxide dose by 10% every 60 seconds. Along with this, the patient should be questioned every 60 to 90 seconds, and any changes in behaviour should be noted. During the process, the patient's legs should not be crossed. This is due to the fact that after sedation is accomplished, the patient seldom moves at all, potentially impairing the appropriate blood flow to the lower extremities. According to studies, a normal inhalation sedation patient needs between 30 and 40 percent nitrous oxide to get the best level of sedation.[1] To begin the dental treatment, establish a level of nitrous oxide and maintain it throughout the procedure. If the planned treatment proceeds without any untoward event, then the sedation is successful.[6,8,9]

Monitoring

When minimal sedatives are used, the individual should be regularly observed for alertness and airway patency.[1] All pharmaceuticals that are administered must have their name, dosage, route, location, and administration time recorded. Continuous monitoring of heart rate, blood pressure, and oxygen saturation is required. Intermittent registration of respiratory rate and blood pressure is also required.[1]

Baseline: A baseline assessment of vital signs must be made before sedative medicines are administered.[1] Blood pressure, heart rate and rhythm, respiration rate, temperature, weight, and height are among the vital indicators that are noted during this pre-treatment visit. These numbers serve as baseline values and ought to be written down in the patient's chart.[5] This might not be possible for certain individuals who are really agitated or uncooperative, thus a note should be made to record this occurrence.

During the procedure: The medical professional must record the brand, dosage, administration location, and time for all drugs used.

- **Regularly checking the pulse** (heart rate and rhythm) every 5 to 15 minutes. The radial artery at the ventral side of the wrist, the brachial artery in the medial antecubital fossa, the carotid artery in the groove between the trachea and the sternocleidomastoid muscle in the neck, or the superficial temporal artery just anterior to the tragus are all places where it can be manually measured. A patient's fingertip or earlobe is used as the site for an electromechanical or optical transducer used in other electronic procedures like pulse monitoring. Following each heartbeat, blood flows through the finger, interrupting a photoelectric beam. A visible or audible signal is produced by this stoppage. ECG is currently widely utilised because it is quite good at detecting dysrhythmias.[6]

ARTERY	LOCATION
Radial	Ventrolateral wrist
Brachial	Medial antecubital fossa
Carotid	Groove between trachea and sternocleidomastoid muscle in neck
Labial	Upper lip
Facial	Cheek
Superficial temporal	Anterior to tragus of ear

Table 10.1 Arteries Employed for Pulse Determination.[6]

- **It's equally critical to keep track of your respiratory health** because the medications used have a depressive effect on the CNS and breathing. Casual monitoring methods, such as seeing the patient's chest rise and fall or the colour of the oral mucous membrane, are unreliable. The precordial/pretracheal stethoscope is very useful for listening to the sounds of breathing and rates per minute. It is crucial to recognise irregular breath sounds since they can suggest a fluid build-up in the upper airway when they imply crackling, bubbling, or gurgling. Suction airways, head tilts, and chin lifts are employed repeatedly to treat it.[6]

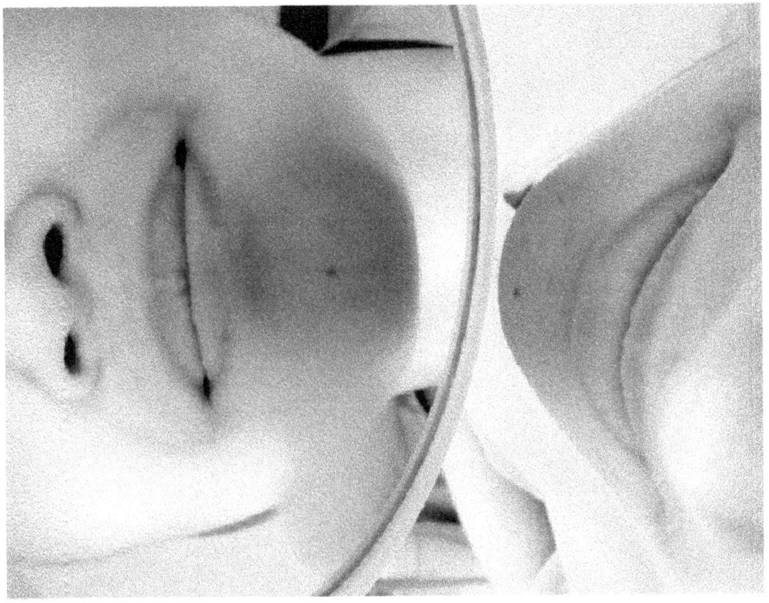

Fig. 10.3 Fogging of mirror indicates exchange of air.[6]

- **Capnography**, a technique for measuring exhaled carbon dioxide that is useful for determining whether there is breathing, whether airways are blocked, and whether there is respiratory depression.

NORMAL CAPNOGRAM

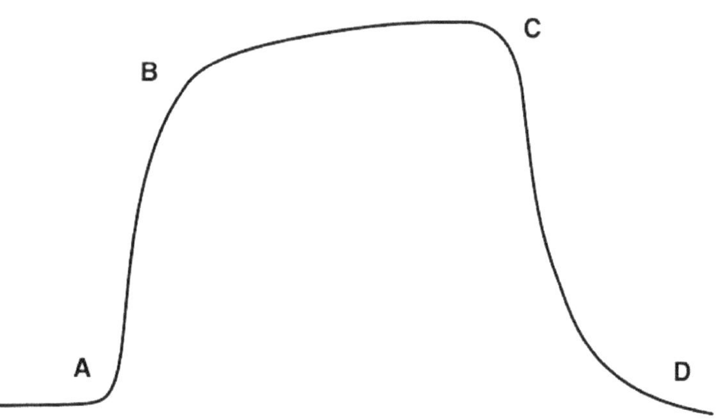

A: Exhalation begins

B-C: Plateau = outflow of alveolar gas

C: End-Tidal CO_2

Fig. 10.4 Normal capnograph.[8]

- **Pulse oximetry** is used to measure oxygen saturation. It calculates how much of a certain wavelength of light is absorbed when it passes through biological tissue. These wavelengths are absorbed by Hb and HbO_2 to varying degrees; the relative percentage of each is determined, and SpO_2 is shown on the screen. 95% SpO_2 is considered normal.[6]

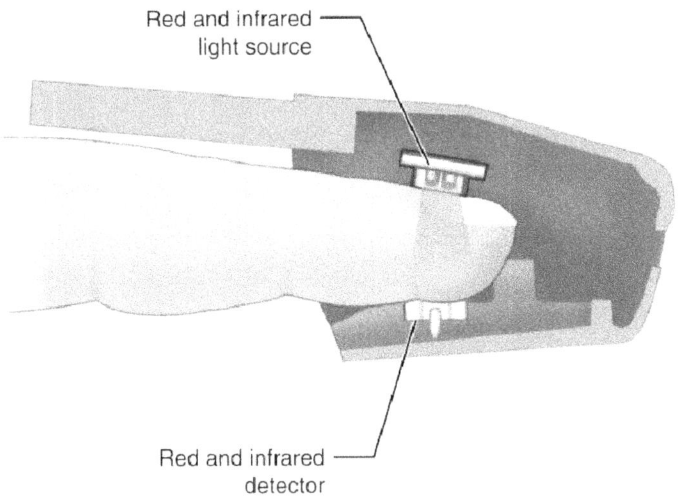

Fig. 10.5 Pulse oximeter measures wavelengths of light passing through the finger.[6]

- **It is not necessary to monitor body temperature**. The most practical method involves placing non-disposable thermometers for three to five minutes under the tongue before reading. There are also digital non-disposable thermometers available.

Fig. 10.6 Noncontact infrared thermometer. (Source: © gettyimages.com.)

- To focus the proper amount of sedation and to quickly identify and react to a deeper level of drowsiness, the **level of consciousness** requires to be continuously monitored. Older children's verbal responses to directives or younger children's reactions to physical stimuli can both be used to gauge a child's level of consciousness. The degree of sedation can be determined by a grading system.[3]

Descriptions	Scores
Patient is anxious and agitated or restless, or both	1
Patient is cooperative, oriented, and tranquil	2
Patient responds to commands only	3
Patient exhibits brisk response to light glabellar tap or loud auditory stimulus	4
Patient exhibits a sluggish response to light glabellar tap or loud auditory stimulus	5
Patient exhibits no response	6

Table 10.2 Ramsay Sedation Scale.[8]

After the procedure

A suitably equipped recovery facility should have functioning suction apparatus, as well as the capacity to deliver more than 90% oxygen and positive pressure ventilation. Patient's vital signs should be recorded at specific intervals. Oxygen saturation and heart monitoring shall be used continuously until appropriate discharge criteria are met.[1]

Sedation records

Each patient using sedative medication requires a written record to be created. These documents serve a variety of functions.

- As a trend diagram of vital values.
- As a memory aid for doctors.
- To record the patient's reaction to the use of medication and the surgical process.
- Not legally but non-clinically as a document.

It includes patient identification, a summary of the preoperative assessment, information on intra-operative monitoring, and information on drug administration. Included are the date, the names of all the medications used, and the procedure's end. The box displays the sedation record issued by the American Academy of Pediatric Dentistry.[1] A crucial element in providing knowledgeable and high-quality oral health treatment is the patient's record. It acts as a resource for information for the patient, the caregiver, and any approved third parties. The recommendation will help the practitioner create and keep an extensive, standardised, and well-organized record of patient treatment.[6,9] It is not, however, meant to establish a standard of treatment.

Date
Name
Pre-op Vitals | BP | HR | SpO_2 | RR
Age | Gender M F | Weight | Height | BMI | Mallampati | ASA
Medical History
NPO
Solids ____ Hours ____ Clear Liquids ____ Hours
Procedure(s)
NIBP L R
Pulse Oximeter
Precordial
ECG
$EtCO_2$
Medications
Operator
Assistants
Drug Allergies
Start | Finish | Premedication | IV 20G 22G
ANES
R L
SURG
Site
TIME
Oxygen (LPM)
Nitrous Oxide (LPM)
Used | Wasted
Midazolam (mg)
Diazepam (mg)
Fentanyl (mcg)
Meperidine (mg)
Hydromorphone (mg)
Sufentanil (mcg)
Ketorolac (mg)
NS (mL)
2% lidocaine 1:100k epi (mg)
4% articaine 1:100k epi (mg)
Response to Verbal Stimuli
SpO_2
Respiratory Rate
$EtCO_2$ Present
ECG Pattern
Discharged to
BP
150
HR
SpO_2
100
RR
☐ Awake
50
☐ Alert
☐ Ambulatory
Comments:

Signature: ____________________

Fig. 10.7 Anesthesia record, which may be used for sedation or general anesthesia.[6]

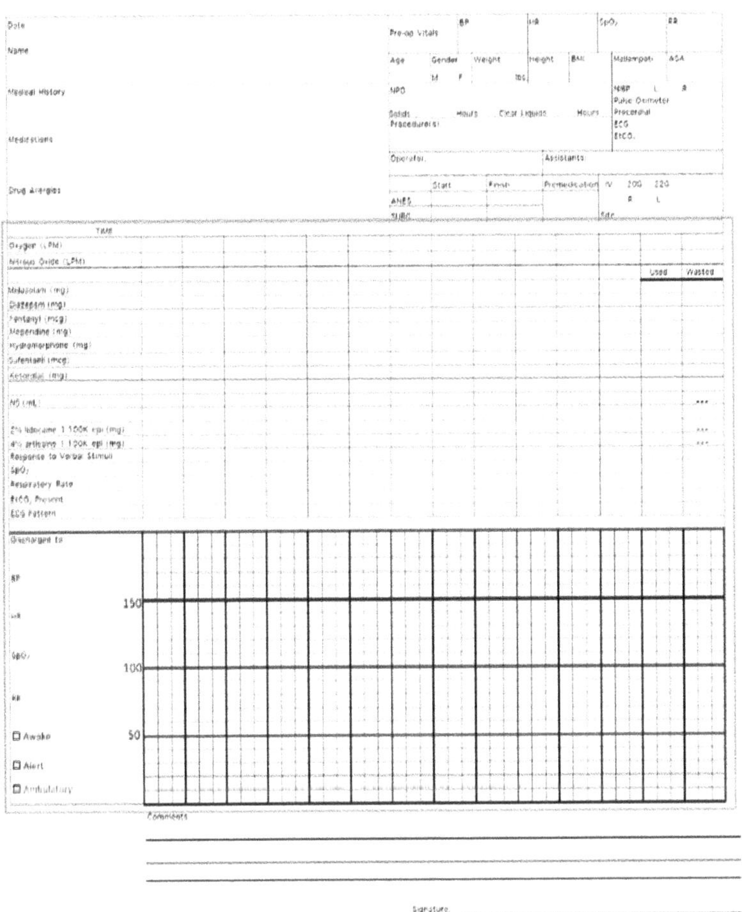

Date

Name

Medical History

Medications

Drug Allergies

Pre-op Vitals | BP | HR | SpO_2 | RR

Age | Gender M F | Weight lbs | Height | BMI | Mallampati | ASA

NPO

Solids ___ Hours ___ Clear Liquids ___ Hours

Procedure(s)

NIBP L R
Pulse Oximeter
Precordial
ECG
$EtCO_2$

Operator | Assistants

| Start | Finish | Premedication | IV 20G 22G R L

ANES

SURG

Site

TIME

Oxygen (LPM)
Nitrous Oxide (LPM)

Used | Wasted

Midazolam (mg)
Diazepam (mg)
Fentanyl (mcg)
Meperidine (mg)
Hydromorphone (mg)
Sufentanil (mcg)
Ketorolac (mg)

NS (mL)

2% lidocaine 1:100K epi (mg)
4% articaine 1:100K epi (mg)
Response to Verbal Stimuli
SpO_2
Respiratory Rate
$EtCO_2$ Present
ECG Pattern

Discharged to

BP

HR

SpO_2

RR

150

100

50

☐ Awake

☐ Alert

☐ Ambulatory

Comments

Signature

Fig. 10.8 Intraoperative monitoring and drug administration data section.[6]

Discharge Criteria

After consuming sedatives, paediatric patients frequently run a high risk of experiencing issues with their airways. Infants‘ sluggish metabolism, delayed drug absorption following oral or rectal administration, the lack of procedural stimulus, decreased monitoring alertness, and infants' poor metabolism are all possible causes of this elevated risk.[2] Following are the recommended criteria to discharge the patient:[3]

- Cardiovascular function is stable and good.
- Satisfactory and uncompromised airway patency
- The individual gets easily aroused and has intact defence mechanisms.
- Adequate hydration level.
- The patient can speak, if applicable.
- If applicable, the patient can sit without assistance.
- The patient, if applicable, can walk with little help.
- The pre-sedation stage of responsiveness, or a level that is as close to it as is practicable for that kid, should be achieved for the child who is extremely young or impaired and incapable of the typically expected reactions.

The following should be completed when considering the discharge of a patient following parenteral sedation. The patient postsedation score must be approximately equal to the baseline (presedation) score.		
Patient's name:	SSN:	Date:
Physical Signs	(Pretreatment)	Baseline/Discharge Comments
A. MOVEMENT 2—able to walk (when appropriate) 1—able to move extremities 0—unable to move any extremity		
B. RESPIRATIONS 2—able to breathe deeply and cough 1—limited respiratory effort 0—no spontaneous respiratory effort		
C. CIRCULATION 2—systolic BP ±20% baseline level 1—systolic BP ±40% baseline level 0—systolic BP > ±40% baseline level		
D. CONSCIOUSNESS 2—full alertness seen in ability to answer questions appropriately 1—aroused when called by name 0—unresponsive to verbal stimulation		
E. COLOR 2—normal skin color and appearance 1—any alteration in skin color 0—frank cyanosis or extreme pale		
TOTAL SCORE: Dr's signature:		

Fig. 10.9 Parenteral sedation discharge criteria.[6]

• • •

References

1. American Academy of Pediatrics, American Academy of Pediatric Dentistry, Coté CJ, Wilson S, Work Group on Sedation. Guidelines for monitoring and management of pediatric patients during and after sedation for diagnostic and therapeutic procedures: an update. Pediatrics. 2006 Dec;118(6):2587-602.
2. Shankar V, Deshpande JK. Procedural sedation in the pediatric patient. Anesthesiology Clinics of North America. 2005 Dec 1;23(4):635-54.
3. Jacob R, Ilamurugu K, Amar N. Paediatric procedural sedation-a review and an update. Indian Journal of Anaesthesia. 2007 May

1;51(3):169-75.

4. American Society of Anesthesiologists. Practice Guidelines for Moderate Procedural Sedation and Analgesia 2018: A Report by the American Society of Anesthesiologists Task Force on Moderate Procedural Sedation and Analgesia, the American Association of Oral and Maxillofacial Surgeons, American College of Radiology, American Dental Association, American Society of Dentist Anesthesiologists, and Society of Interventional Radiology. Anesthesiology. 2018 Mar;128(3):437-79.
5. Folayan MO, Faponle A, Lamikanra A. A review of the pharmacological approach to the management of dental anxiety in children. International journal of paediatric dentistry. 2002 Sep;12(5):347-54.
6. Malamed SF. Sedation-e-book: a guide to patient management. Elsevier Health Sciences; 2017 May 3.
7. Houpt MI, Limb R, Livingston RL. Clinical effects of nitrous oxide conscious sedation in children. Pediatric dentistry. 2004 Jan 1;26(1):29-36.
8. Gupta K, Emmanouil D, Sethi A, editors. Nitrous Oxide in Pediatric Dentistry: a clinical handbook. Springer Nature; 2019 Dec 4.
9. Dean JA, editor. McDonald and Avery's dentistry for the child and adolescent-E-book. Elsevier Health Sciences; 2021 Feb 2.

CHAPTER XI

Clinical And Adverse Effects

Clinical Effects

Individual biovariability explains the various responses and outcomes associated with nitrous oxide inhalation at various doses. Some people's symptoms are severe, while others find them unimportant. Depending on the variability, the visible symptoms may be plain to see or subtle. The doctor must remain exceedingly watchful the entire time the patient is sedated to look for indicators of drowsiness and to distinguish between the good and bad reactions the patient is having. Numerous research has looked at nitrous oxide's physiological, anxiolytic, behavioural, psychomotor, and analgesic effects on juveniles.

1. **Effect on pain sensitivity of the tooth :** In one of the early investigations, conducted in 1944 by Alfred H. Chambers and George G. Schultz, it was shown that breathing nitrous oxide directly affected how painful teeth felt.[1] In this study an upper central incisor was isolated, and patient was made to inhale increasing concentrations of nitrous oxide. The test stimulus given to this was through a high frequency induction shock delivered for testing pulp sensitivity at regular intervals. A significant degree of analgesia was observed at 30–40% nitrous oxide, while analgesia adequate for extraction of tooth was found to be produced by 60% nitrous oxide. This study was one of the early studies where combination sedation and local anaesthesia was not very well known or used. However, the level of analgesia demonstrated was very significant.
2. **Cognitive effects**: Various studies show the effect of nitrous oxide on memory and moods of a person. James P. Zacny et al in

their study categorized patients according to anxiety level into the high, moderate and low anxious individuals who were to get nitrous oxide sedation for dental treatment.[2] It was shown that regardless of the pre – operative anxiety levels, during intake, patients reported a variety of mood-altering responses, the bulk of which were positive. According to scientific research, nitrous oxide may be a useful treatment for easing individual anxiety undergoing dental procedures. Another similar study by **L.M. Thompson et al** showed the effects on cognitive tasks and moods of the patient. They concluded that use of nitrous oxide sedation does not greatly affect superior cognitive skills, thus individuals can return to their regular routines after surgery.[3]

3. **Level of anxiety**: It has been unclear in the past whether the child's anxiety is reduced or whether the child copes with the situation in a better way. **Veerkamp et al** studied the longitudinal dental fear of 55 children who were to be given nitrous oxide sedation for dental procedure. Correlations between the anxiety scores during initial, control and follow – up treatment of highly anxious children suggest that nitrous oxide was a successful agent in influencing anxiety in highly anxious children for a long-term process.[4]
4. **Behaviour of a child**: A child's behaviour during dental treatment is equated with anxiety in the paediatric dentistry literature. The use of nitrous oxide-oxygen gas combinations between 30 and 39 percent drastically changed kids 's behaviour, encouraging them to comply and permit successful dental treatment to be performed.[5]
5. **Objective signs:** It is imperative that the operator recognizes when the desired level of sedation is achieved. This can be done by observing the various body movements and the eyes. A study by Milton I. Houpt et al performed a study on 59 healthy children from ages 4 to 13 years demonstrated the various bodily signs. The inclusion of open hands was the most frequent objective sign observed in 90% of the sample group, followed by limp hindlimbs in 81%. Furthermore, abduction of feet with

toes pointing in lateral direction was also seen. A smile and a trance like state where the child appeared to stare blankly in space was seen in 66% of the children. Laughter with nitrous oxide inhalation was seen only in 14% of the children which was difficult to suppress and control and was characterized as spontaneous in nature.[6] The activity of eye is a very good indicator of the level of sedation. The overall movement may be lessened as patient is unable to focus when sedated.

6. **Subjective symptoms:** Apart from the above-mentioned objective signs, 70% of children also reported with certain subjective symptoms. A general "feeling good" symptom was told by 64% of the patients. Amongst others were drowsiness, sensation in the lips, tingling of extremities, light-headedness, warmth, and heaviness.
7. **Psychomotor effects**: The psychomotor response in the same study was assessed by drawings made by children from the Bender Visual Motor Gestalt Test. It was observed that nitrous oxide above 50% had a small but significant effect on the psychomotor effect of the children.

Adverse Effects

Nitrous oxide has been used as an anaesthetic agent in dentistry for many years. Although its administration in general anaesthesia has reduced over the last few years, the use of nitrous oxide in inhalation sedation has continued till date. It has a good safety record even at higher concentrations of 70%, dentists are rightly concerned with its unwanted effects.[7] According to certain reports, patients are less likely to have negative effects than dentists and dental assistants.[8]

Nitrous oxide has several negative effects, which are categorised as:

- Acute concerning the patient mainly.

- Chronic which can be caused by exposure or abuse.

Mechanism of adverse effects caused by nitrous oxide

Nitrous oxide is no longer regarded as innocuous and causes undesirable effects in addition to hypoxia. It oxidises the reduced form of vitamin B_{12}, or cobalamin, through a chemical reaction with the cobalt-containing metal complexes in our bodies. The development of healthy cells, enzymes, and the operation of our body's many organ systems all depend on vitamin B_{12}.[8]

Factors determining the long-term side effects

Yageila claims that the effects depend on the following factors:[9]

- The quantity and pattern of nitrous oxide exposure.
- The degree to which enzyme synthesis is inhibited and the timeline for recovery.
- The degree to which nutritional intake and physiological reserves counteract the biochemical block brought on by nitrous oxide.
- The metabolic pathway(s) implicated and their sensitivity.
- Sensitivity of the tissue to changed metabolic pathways.

Chronic Adverse Effects

Among the non-specific effects are nausea, perspiration and hallucinations. Nitrous oxide alters the normal functions of the various systems of the body as follows:

1. **Reproductive problems**: The first accounts of the risks of nitrous oxide exposure at work date back to 1967 in Russian literature. It was discovered in the study where anaesthetists were polled that long-term exposure to anaesthetic gases had an impact on reproduction. Long-term exposure to nitrous oxide has been found to increase the number of miscarriages. Reduced fertility was noted in males. It was asserted that the likelihood of pregnancy following each menstrual cycle decreased by 6% for every hour of exposure to nitrous oxide. The number of congenital abnormalities in the exposed anaesthetists' children increased was also observed.[8] There is proof that exposure is linked to a higher rate of spontaneous abortion and a longer gestation period.
2. **Neurological defects**: Chronic exposure causes a multitude of neurological abnormalities in both male and female dental team members. It has been demonstrated that the spinal cord can experience subacute combined degeneration over time.[8]
3. **Haematological and immunological problems**: Studies done on the bone marrow of dentists who habitually used nitrous oxide in their operatories and patients who received nitrous oxide sedation showed direct depression of Vitamin B_{12} which caused bone marrow changes. These changes occur through the abnormal methionine synthetase activity which causes impaired synthesis of DNA in the bone marrow, leading to megaloblastic anaemia like changes.[10,11]
4. **Liver problems:** According to Cohen et al., extensively exposed male dentists had a 1 to7 fold increase in liver disease incidence, whereas heavily exposed female dentists had a 1 to 5 fold increase compared to their non-exposed counterparts.
5. **Kidney problems**: Renal calculi were more common, which was the main factor contributing to the growth in kidney diseases in men. There has been an increase in genito-urinary tract infections in women.
6. **Malignancy**: Nitrous oxide was first shown to be teratogenic in 1967.[12] Animal studies have confirmed these findings that

chronic exposure to high level of nitrous oxide produces teratogenic effects in rats and that this effect can be partially reduced or controlled by supplementing with folinic acid. Additionally, reports of a 2- to 4-fold increase in the frequency of cervical cancer among female dental assistants have been made, showing a higher rate of malignancy because of exposure.[8]

7. **Fetotoxicity**: In 1986, Nunn and Chanarin highlighted the fetotoxicity of nitrous oxide in research on animals and proposed that using it as an anaesthetic in the first and second trimesters of pregnancy would pose a risk. Early pregnancy procedures performed under nitrous oxide sedation may cause a spontaneous abortion. Other non-fatal abnormalities that were found in the infants of the chronically exposed participants were nevi, haemangiomas, and hydroceles.[11]
8. **Wound healing**: Nitrous oxide exposure impairs the synthesis of DNA, which can disrupt tissues going through rapid cell cycle. It was hypothesised that since this form of cell division takes place while a wound heals, nitrous oxide could have a negative or slowing influence on how quickly the lesion heals. However, animal tests that measured the strength of a healed wound (via a rupture test) did not reveal any appreciably different results because of exposure to nitrous oxide.[13]
9. **Environmental effects**: Concerns have also been expressed over nitrous oxide's impact on the aerosphere, its role in the greenhouse effect, and the ozone layer's deterioration. Despite the fact that nitrous oxide certainly play a role in these occurrences, anaesthesiologists who care about the environment can rest easy knowing that anaesthetic-related nitrous oxide accounts for only 1% of the agent's total global production, which accounts for only 0.5% of the greenhouse impact.[14]
10. **Psychomotor impairment**: When adult volunteers were exposed to as minimal as 50 ppm N_2O over a duration of two hours, it was found that their psychomotor function on tasks involving sense of sight, short-term memory, reasoning, and

motor responses was impaired.This cannot be directly concluded due to the flaws in such studies related to patient perception, subjective symptoms and level of sedation, hence it is impossible to state whether there can occur an irreversible psychomotor impairment due to nitrous oxide exposure.[15]

Acute Sedation Events

There have been various studies published with the immediate side effects to patients receiving nitrous oxide sedation in terms of complications and adverse events. One such study by William et al in 2001 showed that nausea and vomiting with a feeling of dizziness was the most common side effect of nitrous oxide sedation alone or in combination with other drugs. Others were the respiratory depressive effects causing apnea and oxygen desaturation. Concerns over the recovery period and discharge have been emphasized in the past, which is why, another such finding was a prolonged sedation and slow recovery time observed in some patients. Though such events are not always avoidable, under a strict protocol and use of O_2 supplementation, these can be minimized to a great extent.[16]

Minimizing the risk

The National Institute for Occupational Safety and Health (NIOSH) established threshold standards for N_2O exposure at work in the 1970s. Scavenging systems were developed and initially considered effective at reducing waste N_2O concentration levels to the 25ppm NIOSH recommendation. However, many studies indicate that even in the presence of scavenging devices ambient N_2O levels routinely exceed NIOSH recommendations.[17,18]

To further reinforce the importance of reducing the ambient N_2O levels to 25ppm, various policies of ADA and AAPD state that-

- Employ scavenging devices that eliminate nitrous oxide as the patient exhales.
- Ensure that scavenged air and gases are properly vented through exhaust systems away from fresh air intakes and to the building's exterior.
- Ventilate dentist offices using only fresh outdoor air.
- Conduct thorough, routine maintenance on the nitrous oxide/oxygen supply systems.
- Think carefully before selecting a patient to administer nitrous oxide.
- Each patient should have a mask that fits them appropriately, and throughout administration, you should keep an eye on the patient and titrate the flow or percentage of nitrous oxide to the lowest effective level.
- While administering nitrous oxide, urge patients to speak and breathe through their mouths as little as possible.
- When possible, use a rubber dam and high-volume oral aspiration.
- After the procedure is finished, give the patient 100% oxygen for at least five minutes to clear the nitrous oxide delivery system.

• • •

References

1. Chambers AH, Schultz GG. Effect of subanesthetic nitrous oxide—oxygen mixtures on pain sensitivity of the tooth. Journal of Dental Research. 1945 Feb;24(1):1-5.
2. Zacny JP, Hurst RJ, Graham L, Janiszewski DJ. Preoperative dental anxiety and mood changes during nitrous oxide inhalation. The Journal of the American Dental Association. 2002 Jan 1;133(1):82-8.

3. Thompson JM, Neave N, Moss MC, Scholey AB, Wesnes K, Girdler NM. Cognitive properties of sedation agents: comparison of the effects of nitrous oxide and midazolam on memory and mood. British Dental Journal. 1999 Nov;187(10):557-62.
4. Veerkamp JS, Gruythuysen RJ, Hoogstraten J, Van Amerongen WE. Anxiety reduction with nitrous oxide: a permanent solution?. ASDC journal of dentistry for children. 1995 Jan 1;62(1):44-8.
5. Mamoon Fnaish BD. Nitrous oxide oxygen inhalation sedation in pediatric dentistry. JRMS. 2010 Mar;17(1):38-42.
6. Houpt MI, Limb R, Livingston RL. Clinical effects of nitrous oxide conscious sedation in children. Pediatric dentistry. 2004 Jan 1;26(1):29-36.
7. Babl FE, Oakley E, Seaman C, Barnett P, Sharwood LN. High-concentration nitrous oxide for procedural sedation in children: adverse events and depth of sedation. Pediatrics. 2008 Mar;121(3):e528-32.
8. Donaldson D, Meechan JG. The hazards of chronic exposure to nitrous oxide: an update. British dental journal. 1995 Feb;178(3):95-100.
9. Yagiela JA. Health hazards and nitrous oxide: a time for reappraisal. Anesthesia progress. 1991 Jan;38(1):1.
10. Sweeney B, Bingham RM, Amos RJ, Petty AC, Cole PV. Toxicity of bone marrow in dentists exposed to nitrous oxide. Br Med J (Clin Res Ed). 1985 Aug 31;291(6495):567-9.
11. Nunn JF, Chanarin I, Tanner AG, Owen ER. Megaloblastic bone marrow changes after repeated nitrous oxide anaesthesia: reversal with folinic acid. BJA: British Journal of Anaesthesia. 1986 Dec 1;58(12):1469-70.
12. Keeling PA, Rocke DA, Nunn JF, Monk SJ, Lumb MJ, Halsey MJ. Folinic acid protection against nitrous oxide teratogenicity in the rat. British Journal of Anaesthesia. 1986 May 1;58(5):528-34.
13. Aligie T, Seth A, Barbenel JC, Galloway DJ, Gray WM, Spence AA. Nitrous oxide and wound healing. BJA: British Journal of

Anaesthesia. 1985 Jun 1;57(6):621-3.

14. SHERMAN SJ, CULLEN BF. Nitrous oxide and the greenhouse effect. The Journal of the American Society of Anesthesiologists. 1988 May 1;68(5):816-7.
15. Moore PA. Psychomotor impairment due to N2O exposure. Anesthesia Progress. 1983 May;30(3):72.
16. Leelataweedwud P, Vann Jr WF. Adverse events and outcomes of conscious sedation for pediatric patients: study of an oral sedation regimen. The Journal of the American Dental Association. 2001 Nov 1;132(11):1531-9.
17. Boiano JM, Steege AL. Precautionary practices for administering anesthetic gases: A survey of physician anesthesiologists, nurse anesthetists and anesthesiologist assistants. Journal of occupational and environmental hygiene. 2016 Oct 2;13(10):782-93.
18. Boiano JM, Steege AL, Sweeney MH. Exposure control practices for administering nitrous oxide: A survey of dentists, dental hygienists, and dental assistants. Journal of Occupational and Environmental Hygiene. 2017 Jun 3;14(6):409-16.

CHAPTER XII

Present And Future Of Nitrous Oxide

There is no denying that the opinions calling for the scientific community and the medical society to look past nitrous oxide have become louder in consecutive years. The environmental risks linked with its use are one of the reasons behind this. We'll look at a few of them in this section.

Ironically, the health sector themselves are the top emitter of carbon dioxide, despite the World Health Organization's recent declaration that climate change is the "defining issue for health systems" in this century. According to the WHO, approximately 0.3% of all deaths are thought to be related to climate change, and this percentage is projected to rise in the years to come. The rise in chest illnesses, asthma attacks, and cardiovascular disorders may be related to the deteriorating air quality. Our future and existence may be threatened by rising temperatures, which may hasten the spread of infectious diseases, melt glaciers, and raise ocean levels. Thus, it makes sense for us to reduce our adverse effects on the environment.[1,2]

Role of nitrous oxide in depleting ozone layer

Numerous research has already emphasised how important nitrous oxide is to the greenhouse impact. In a 1976 paper that appeared in Science, the authors examined the greenhouse impact brought on by trace gases and specifically examined the roles that nitrous oxide, methane, and ammonia played.[3] The largest source of nitrous oxide in the atmosphere, according to the authors of that research, is the breakdown of organic waste and fertilisers. Most nitrous oxide emissions into the atmosphere, or about 70%, are caused by microorganisms in the soil and ocean breaking down nitrogen. The remaining 30% of nitrous oxide emissions are brought on by human activities such as agriculture, fertiliser use, and the growth of crops that fix nitrogen.

The scope and quantity of the activities we engaged in that contributed to the atmospheric concentration of nitrous oxide increased significantly between 1976 and the present, however, and what was considered a trace substance in 1976 became dominant. In 2009, a paper titled Nitrous Oxide: The Dominant Ozone-Depleting Substance Emitted in the 21st Century was published in the same journal, *Science*. This research, as well as numerous others that have been published since, have highlighted the growing contribution of nitrous oxide to having a harmful environmental impact.[3,4]

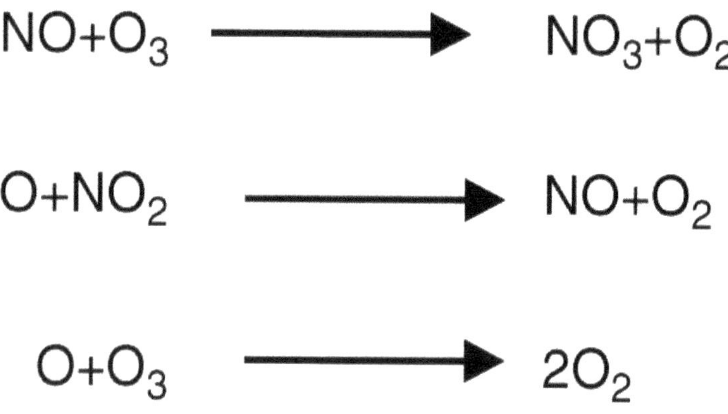

Fig. 11.1 Chemical reaction which forms the basis of "destruction of ozone" by nitrogen oxides.[6]

Role of Nitrous Oxide in Causing Global Warming

There are certain rules on restricting the extravasation of anaesthetic gases, including nitrous oxide, into the atmosphere[5]. Nitrous oxide's role as an operating room pollutant and its detrimental effects on staff have been investigated meticulously. The currently inhaled anaesthetic gases go through very little metabolic processing in the body before being expelled and scavenged by the anaesthetic machine, where they are vented out with very minimal deterioration. These are long-lasting greenhouse gases that stay in the atmosphere. Due to its function as a carrier gas when delivering more vigorous anaesthetic gases like sevoflurane and desflurane, nitrous oxide's importance as a greenhouse gas increases in the treatment room as opposed to a dental clinic. Because desflurane has a strong capacity to trap heat and nitrous oxide is emitted in enormous quantities and remains in the atmosphere for an extended period, the combination of the two has an even greater impact.[5]

Therefore, nitrous oxide damages the ozone layer and raises the possibility of global warming. All of the aforementioned data point to the need for anaesthesiologists and dentists to consider techniques to use and release less nitrous gas into the atmosphere. One suggestion is

1. To avoid using high fresh gas flows unless necessary.
2. Nitrous oxide and desflurane should only be used together in circumstances where doing so may lower mortality and morbidity.

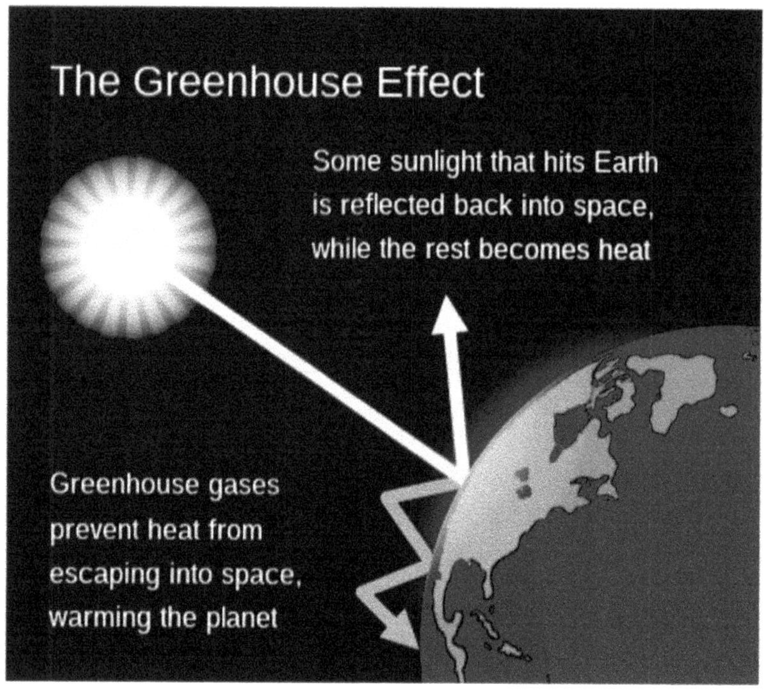

Fig. 11.2 The Greenhouse Effect

New technologies that could purify or destroy anaesthetic gases have been developed in the exclusion of any regulations on the release of used anaesthetic gases into the atmosphere. These include "Deltasorb," which employs a canister that gets connected to an existing scavenging circuit and subsequently adsorbs volatile anaesthetic gases, and photochemical air purification, which may "theoretically destroy all waste anaesthetic gases". The seller receives these canisters and transforms the seized anaesthetics into medical grade anaesthetics by extracting, liquifying, and purifying them.[55] When completely developed and implemented, technologies like these will aid in reducing the negative effects of anaesthetic gas emission into the atmosphere.

Due to heightened awareness of the occurrence of procedural-related anxiety and pain in even the infants, paediatric procedural sedation has developed quickly during the past ten years. The development of new paradigms for safe, effective, and resource-efficient systems of providing procedural sedation has been sparked by the increased demands in a variety of situations, new definitions of the levels of sedation, new regulatory requirements, and the development of short-acting titratable sedatives. It is crucial to intervene using non-invasive methods that offer a secure, child-focused environment and timely opportunities for individuals to experience and manage frightening circumstances.

Numerous patients, including youngsters, have benefited from the use of nitrous oxide since without this helpful adjunct, they would either have stopped receiving dental care altogether or would have been forced to undergo "general anaesthesia" each time they needed even basic dental care. In order to securely enable effective treatment, reduce or remove the need for punitive measures, and help a kid deficient in cooperative capacity transition to the phase when cooperation potential develops, sedation techniques are routinely employed to obtund aggressive and potentially dangerous behaviours. Nitrous oxide's history shows us that it has enormous analgesic and anxiety-relieving potential and will continue to play a crucial role in dentistry.

• • •

References

1. Chung JW, Meltzer DO. Estimate of the carbon footprint of the US health care sector. JAMA. 2009;302:1970.
2. World Health Organization. Protecting health from climate change, 2009. http://whqlibdoc. who.int/publications/2009/9789241598880_eng.pdf

3. Wang WC, Yung LY, Lacis AA, Mo T, Hansen JE. Green house effects due to manmade perturbation soft race gases. Science. 1976;194(4266):685–90
4. Ravishankara AR, Daniel SJ, Portmann WR. Nitrous oxide : the dominant ozone-depleting substance emitted in the 21st century. Science. 2009;326(5949):123–5
5. Gupta K, Emmanouil D, Sethi A, editors. Nitrous Oxide in Pediatric Dentistry: a clinical handbook. Springer Nature; 2019 Dec 4.
6. Ravishankara AR, Daniel JS, Portmann RW. Nitrous oxide (N2O): the dominant ozone-depleting substance emitted in the 21st century. science. 2009 Oct 2;326(5949):123-5.

CHAPTER XIII

Conclusion

Due to heightened awareness of the occurrence of procedural-related anxiety and pain in even the youngest children, paediatric procedural sedation has developed quickly during the past ten years. The development of new paradigms of safe, effective, and resource-efficient systems of providing procedural sedation has been sparked by the increased demands in a variety of situations, new definitions of the levels of sedation, new regulatory requirements, and the development of short-acting titratable sedatives. It is crucial to intervene using non-invasive methods that offer a secure, child-focused environment and timely opportunities for individuals to experience and manage frightening circumstances.

Numerous patients, including youngsters, have benefited from the use of nitrous oxide since without this helpful adjunct, they would either have stopped receiving dental care altogether or would have been forced to undergo "general anaesthesia" every time they needed even basic dental care.

Sedation techniques can frequently be used to obtund disruptive and potentially harmful behaviours to safely permit quality care, minimise or eliminate the need for punitive measures, and assist a child lacking in cooperative ability in making the transition to the stage when cooperation potential develops. The history of nitrous oxide shows us that it has tremendous analgesic and anxiolytic potential and that it will always be used in dentistry.

• • •

www.ingramcontent.com/pod-product-compliance
Ingram Content Group UK Ltd.
Pitfield, Milton Keynes, MK11 3LW, UK
UKHW021658190726
13853UKWH00001B/342

9 798887 832692